MW00909140

Completely

a call to live fully surrendered

Jackie Policastro

WestBow Press books may be ordered through booksellers or by contacting:

WestBow Press
A Division of Thomas Nelson & Zondervan
1663 Liberty Drive
Bloomington, IN 47403
www.westbowpress.com
1 (866) 928-1240

ISBN: 978-1-5127-5063-8 (sc)
ISBN: 978-1-5127-5065-2 (hc)
ISBN: 978-1-5127-5064-5 (e)

Library of Congress Control Number: 2016911914

Print information available on the last page.

WestBow Press rev. date: 8/25/2016

Contents

Dedication

To my brother, Jake Lloyd
Not only were we able to overcome the
"Cain" within us (thus sparing each other's
lives) but we are each other's keeper!
Beyond that, I am thankful to have grown up
with such an artsy-genius as you. I love you!

And to all those who have yet to overcome the
"Cain" within them - if you give yourself to
God completely, will He not complete you?

Foreword

Hello Friend,

My name is Ryan Daniel. I am the singer for a band called "Among The Thirsty" and I am the composer and author of a song called "Completely." When Jackie asked me to write this foreword for her book, I was very humbled. Not to mention the fact that the title of the book was inspired by a song I had written. Before you delve into the truth and experiences written on these pages, I want to start out by saying this is my first time writing a foreword for a book, so bear with me.

Surrender. A word that is synonymous with defeat. Merriam-Webster's Collegiate Dictionary defines "surrender" as: "to agree to stop fighting, hiding, resisting, etc., because you know that you will not win or succeed" or "to give up control…"[1] It's a painful word, it's a painful experience because, simply put, it feels like we are losing. Surrender is both a noun and a verb. It's something that exists, but it's also a word that requires action. We are required to make the choice, to lay down our arms, lay down who we are, even our dreams. Again, all of this doesn't sound comfortable or fun to say the least, but what if you surrendered to someone who had more love for you than you could fathom? What if you surrendered to someone who knows your beginning, middle and end? What if you surrendered to someone who absolutely wanted nothing but the best for you?

As you journey through Jackie's book, you are going to see that surrender is just that: A journey. Sure, there are certainly powerful moments in our lives where we surrender things we thought we couldn't live without. My song "Completely" is about that very thing, but there is so much more to it than that! Surrender goes beyond a single act. Surrender is a daily exercise, like jogging or eating right, to maintain our health. Learning to surrender daily will give us healthy hearts, a healthy spirit, and most importantly, a clear view of who God is, who you are to Him and how much He loves you.

Surrender is hard. Surrender is painful. It feels as if we are losing, but when we surrender to the God of the universe who knows our every breath, and knows every hair on our head, we are ultimately saying: "I can't do this, help me!" This is one of the bravest things anyone can do. I hope this book helps you on your surrender journey. I hope it takes you to places that make you uncomfortable, and places that make you see the truth beyond the veil of self we place over our hearts.

Lastly, I want you to imagine the day of the crucifixion. The day Jesus breathed his last breath. Imagine that from the eyes of the disciples. I mean, just try to imagine what they were thinking! As far as they were concerned, the ride was over. They were finished. Their hope died with Jesus on the cross. However, that was not the end of the story. Three days later, Jesus rose from the grave, conquering death, and transforming the wrath of God into unending grace.

Surrender is very similar to the events that transpired the day the disciples saw their Jesus hang on a cross. Therefore, remember this:

Surrender only looks like defeat.

Ryan Daniel

Chapter 1

In the Beginning

The Beginning, The End

In the beginning God created… (Genesis 1:1a)

I am Alpha and Omega, the beginning and the end, the first and the last. (Revelation 22:13)

Then you will call, and the LORD will answer; You will cry, and He will say, "Here I am." (Isaiah 58:9a NASB)

Who I Am

It was the fall of 2000 and I was a seventeen-year-old girl headed off to a new beginning: my first semester of college over twelve hundred miles from home. I wasn't sure I wanted to go, but I knew I needed to.

The next several weeks consisted of the typical things: getting to know my roommates, meeting new friends, learning the layout of the campus and getting settled into classes.

As much as the semester days ahead of me should have been exciting and enjoyable, I found myself a little lost inside and out. There's something about that time of life in particular that can get a person thinking and re-evaluating. It's almost a "quarter-life crisis" if you will. Being far from home, family and comforts only enhanced this crisis and Satan took full advantage.

Doubts and questions filled my mind. Confusion and chaos flooded my heart. I began to wonder who I was and what I was doing. Did I really believe God and all that He says He is?

I have to admit that I'm the kind of person who likes the lines clearly defined. It's either black or white. If I'm in, I'm going all in. When the thick, gray clouds blew my way, I needed to make up my mind. I needed to know in my heart which way I was going and who I really was.

More time passed by and I was as low as ever. Satan's manipulative questions were echoing within me and God seemed to be nowhere. In the meantime, I tried to keep myself busy by joining a soccer team at the college. I played striker left wing. Games were held behind the girls' dorm, with one goal facing the dorm while the other goal faced a wide-open field.

On one particular game night on that field, our team was really struggling to maintain any hope of winning. Okay—we were getting crushed! I'd had enough. Wasn't that right where my heart was too? Little hope. Little faith. Little me. Crushed!

I attempted another goal on the field end. The ball was intercepted and flew back toward the dorm end of the field in what seemed like milliseconds. I didn't move. I was still at the field end looking up at the stars. Through frustration, tears and an out-of-breath voice, I let out the words, "God, where are You?" It was a cry of desperation; one last attempt for help.

I did not expect an answer. My faith was as small as a speck. Yet, God kindly spoke three astounding words into my heart.

"Here, I AM" came His reply.

What? Did I really just hear Him? Did He really speak? Yes. Yes, I heard Him. No audible voice, just a word to my heart. His "Here, I AM" was clear and there is no doubt that the "I AM" was uppercase. It was as if He was saying, "I AM is here."

There was nothing left to do but bow down in total surrender. A flood washed over me. It was a flood that overcame my confusion and doubt. It was a recollection of who He is, who He was, the One who is to come. He immersed me in Himself, encompassed me with His mercy and cradled me in His arms. I was His baby—and I still am.

It's hard to describe how it all happened that day. I continued the soccer game and as I recall, we still lost. I was never called offside, nor did anyone ever ask where I was or what I was doing in those moments in the middle of the game.

All I know is I cried out to God in a desperate state and He met me there. The One who created the brightly lit stars above had spoken to me. He spoke *comfort* with words of *existence* and yet revealed *power* with words of *identity.* Because He told me who *He* was, I was able to decipher who *I* was.

I... am... *completely...* His!

The Creator of Me

To understand our true identity, we have to go all the way back to the beginning. If we don't know where we came from, we cannot be sure of where we are going. We must establish our starting point if we want to confirm our finish. **The Beginning, The End**. In other words, the beginning tells us about the end. They have a connection.

Genesis chapter 1 launches the words that describe the beginning by saying, "In the beginning God…" (1:1a). Within the first four words of the Bible, we learn that God is Alpha. He is the beginning. To say that He is Alpha, who originally existed by Himself, is difficult to fathom. What we can humanly grasp is that there was nothing and no one before Him.

By reading on to the next word, *created*, and the following verses that describe what God created, we meet Him as *our* Maker. Genesis 1:26a informs us how *our* beginning began: "And God said, Let *us* make man in *our* image, after *our* likeness" (emphasis added). The "us" and "our" refer to the Father, Son and Holy Spirit. It is not just God the Father at the scene when the foundations of the world are laid. Jesus and the Holy Spirit are right there existing as one with the Father.

God (the three persons in one) created man in His image. The best way to understand what the "image of God" actually means is to look at New Testament passages that describe our restoration back to our original image. Ephesians 4:24 says, "And put on the new self, which in the *likeness of God* has been created in *righteousness* and *holiness* of truth" (NASB; emphasis added). Colossians 3:10 describes the new self as "renewed to a true *knowledge* according to the *image of the One who created him*" (NASB; emphasis added). In these verses, the image of God refers to God's character, holiness and righteousness. We were created with pure and genuine attributes. We were created without a single touch of evil in mind, heart and action. What beauty!

> **God created us in the perfect and beautiful image of Himself!**

After God created the first man in His image (Adam), He said, "*It* is not good that man should be alone; I will make him a help meet for him" (Genesis 2:18). God caused Adam to sleep and removed one of his ribs, which He used to form Eve.

Adam was made one flesh with woman. They were right for each other; they were fit for each other; and they completed each other. Not only that, but they began a perfect relationship with each other because they communed perfectly with God.

At this point in the story of Adam and Eve, all was good. The world was astounding. The first two people were indescribably beautiful inside and out. They were complete. I wish we could park here a bit longer, but we both know that the reality in which we currently live is due to what came next in the story. The next part explains why we were born with identity issues.

The Identity Thief

It was not long after creation that Adam and Eve fell from their perfect communion with God and reaped the consequences of their actions, which in turn affected the whole world. Romans 5:12 describes this effect by saying, "Wherefore, as by one man sin entered into the world, and death by sin; and so death passed upon all men, for that all have sinned."

How did this all happen? We learn in 1 John 3:8 that "the devil has sinned since the beginning" (NASB). Revelation 12 speaks of a war that broke out in heaven. This war was between Michael and his angels and the Dragon and his angels. The Dragon and his angels could not prevail and were thrown out of heaven to the earth. Just in case we needed further clarification of who this dragon was, verse 9 follows up with, "that old serpent, called the Devil, and Satan, which deceiveth the whole world."

So, when did the Dragon get thrown to the earth? In Genesis 1:1, we know that "in the beginning God created the heaven and the earth." The Bible accounts six days of creation with the phrase "and God saw that it was good" at the end of each day (Genesis 1:10 NASB). We can easily conclude that it would not have been good if the Dragon was on the earth at this point.

Therefore, the Dragon, Satan, was likely thrown down sometime after day seven. Though six days were declared as good, the seventh day was declared holy. He could not have been thrown down too long after this, because Adam and Eve were obedient to God's command to be fruitful and multiply—and we know that the Serpent deceived them before they had children.

Since the moment Satan was thrown to the earth, he had a mission to steal the identity of humankind. Since he loved himself so much, he wanted humankind to carry *his* image instead of God's. Unfortunately, Satan's operation was successful. But how in the world did he do it? How did he get humankind to fall for another image?

Remember that Satan is subtle. He is not holding up a sign that says "Honk twice for Satan," "Vote for Satan" or "Drive this way for Satan Lane." He is most likely to mix a bit of God's truth with his lies—or even a bit of his lies with a lot of God's truth.

He will not approach you as the wolf that he is, but rather will show up in a cute and cuddly sheep costume. In an attempt to get you to change *your* image, Satan disguises his *own* image in order to trick you. In Eve's case, Satan showed up by entering a snake.

Our idea of the snake today is not so impressive but that is based in part on Eve's experience. Since sin, death and curses had not yet entered the world, Satan actually showed up through a good thing that God had created. How subtle he truly is!

The snake in the garden was not as the snake looks today since the curse changed its image. In fact, all of the cattle and beasts of the field were cursed, but the snake was cursed above them all (Genesis 3:14). Though the image of animal and man were both affected by the curse, there are major differences between the image that animal and man were *originally* created in. We were designed (both internally and externally) differently from one another.

Since it was Satan's goal to confuse man about his image, it is crucial to know how man's image was created different from the animal image through which Satan spoke to man. One of the main differences between man and animals is the way in which the two began to breathe. The Hebrew word *nephesh*, meaning "a soul, living being…"[2], is used in the Genesis passages about both man and animal, but only man was created by God breathing *His* breath of life into him. God was personal with man.

God Himself formed man from the dust of the ground, breathed into him His breath, and because of that, "man became a living soul" (Genesis 2:7b). Man was not a body walking around before the breath of God. It was the intimate breath of God that made man alive.

On the other hand, animals were created by God's

spoken word which said, "Let the earth bring forth the living creature" (Genesis 1:24).

In other differences, man was created in the image of God and animals were not. Man has free-will and animals do not. Man can choose a relationship with Jesus Christ and be called a child of God. This simply does not apply to animals. There are several other differences, but the last one that must be stated is that man was given authority over animals by God.

Animals were certainly a good thing that God created, but they were not created in His image. It hardly seems like coincidence that Satan showed up in the Garden of Eden through an animal. Perhaps, metaphorically, Satan wanted to show up in the image that he wanted to reduce man to.

You see, Satan wants you to deny that God breathed His breath of life into you. He wants you to believe that your origin evolved from a creature. He wants you to reject the offer of becoming God's child. He wants you to refuse a relationship with Jesus. He wants you to believe that the creatures God gave you rule over, are in equal or higher position than you.

It appears that Satan's goal is to get man to believe in a *subtraction* of his original image. He wants to *devalue* man to the characteristics of an animal—not just any animal, but a cursed, wild, brute beast that is irresponsible, uncontrollable and without reason. Satan wants to convince you of a *subtraction* of your image so you will take on his image as an *addition*. In order to convince you of a subtraction of your identity, Satan must first get you to believe in a subtraction of God's identity!

Look at what the serpent said to Eve: "Indeed, has God said, 'You shall not eat from any tree of the garden'?" (Genesis 3:1 NASB). Here, Satan attempted to get Eve to believe that God is mean—the subtraction that He is good.

In other words, Satan was saying, "Is God really denying you the enjoyment of this garden?"

A few lines later, the serpent contradicted what God said about the punishment of Adam and Eve if they were to disobey. He said, "You surely will not die!" (Genesis 3:4 NASB). This was Satan trying to convince Eve that God is a liar—the subtraction that He is truthful. Satan was saying that God was less than who He said He was.

If God's words weren't true concerning the tree and punishment, then God's words may not be true concerning who is Alpha and Creator. Satan wanted man to dismiss the identity of God from the beginning so that man would dismiss his own identity from the beginning. He wanted man to question the true image of God so that man would be confused about the true image of himself. The result? Eve ended up believing the *lies of the created* over the *truth of the Creator*! She believed the crafty speech of Satan through an animal (which man was given dominion over—Genesis 1:28).

Next, Satan offered Eve an *addition*. It was the addition of what Eve thought was wisdom and power. He said, "you will be like God" (Genesis 3:5 NASB). Satan convinced Eve that there was something to gain. He wanted her to believe that there was another image out there that was better than the one she already had. He was also diminishing God's identity by getting Eve to mentally envision attaining the same supremacy as God.

Satan's lies to Eve planted doubt in her identity and desire for more than her identity and she literally ate it up. What an addition this was! Adam also traded his identity as he too ate the forbidden fruit. The addition got bigger and bigger—but not better and better! All Adam and Eve ended up acquiring was the misery, worry, confusion, anxiety, frustration and shame that arose from sin and the hurry to hide it.

Satan's lies switched the order of authorities. God is the ruler over all and He gave humankind authority over the animals. Satan suggested that humankind could be as wise as God and that the particular animal (the Serpent) through which Satan spoke was wiser than humankind. Satan's lies subtly placed himself in the Alpha position all while letting Eve believe that she was the one benefiting!

After Adam and Eve fell for the lies of the identity thief, they sewed fig leaves together to cover their loins. They attempted to clothe their shame through the works of their own hands. Isaiah 30:1 says, "Woe to the rebellious children, saith the LORD, that take counsel, but not of me; and that cover with a covering, but not of my spirit, that they may add sin to sin." Adam and Eve took the wrong advice and were desperate to cover up their shameful image which no longer reflected innocence.

In all the years since Adam and Eve, Satan's desires and tactics haven't changed. Even today, Satan wants people to remain in the sinful image they were born into. He wants to keep them believing in a subtraction of their original identity. He wants to add "sin to sin" in their lives. He wants them confused about who is the true Alpha.

Even though man cannot escape physical death, he *can* escape spiritual death by trusting in Jesus Christ. Satan wants to keep man from experiencing spiritual life. Satan wants to keep unbelievers living vulnerable and subject to the unruly, wild beast of an owner that he truly is.

We cannot escape ownership. We can only make the choice to have a different master! Choosing your master is choosing what *image* you want as an end result. Do you want to remain with an identity that generates crisis, consequence and uncertainty of who you are, or obtain an identity that promises assurance, reward and purpose? It's time to choose between staying with the one who fraudulently *stole* your identity or being swept away with the One who can completely and eternally *restore* it.

Oh—and just in case you hadn't heard, the *identity restorer* already crushed the head of the *identity thief*! He even preplanned it!

The Preplanned Redemption of Me

The preplanned redemption existed long before sin. It wasn't a whimsical idea that popped into God's head. It wasn't something that God made up after being surprised by sin. No. God was not (nor is He ever) surprised! God knew the future (Matthew 25:34, Ephesians 1:4-5).

> **Our redemption was planned before we ever fell for the lies of the thief!**

The preplanned redemption was first spoken of *between* the punishment of the serpent and the punishment of humankind. After God cursed the serpent, but before He punished Adam and Eve, He declared His plan to redeem humankind by saying that a Seed (that is, Jesus) would bruise Satan's head (Genesis 3:15). God's declaration to rescue man came *before* the punishment of man!

Sure, man would be punished in the following verse, but God's mercy, the One called Jesus, declared Salvation *first*. God's statement to the serpent demonstrated who was in charge and who wasn't, who had been telling the truth and who had been lying, and who would win in the end and who would be defeated!

Jeremiah 29:11 says, "For I know the thoughts that I think toward you, saith the LORD, thoughts of peace, and not of evil, to give you an expected end." His thoughts toward us were good from the beginning because He was thinking about the end. Adam and Eve's actions would need a present punishment, but God wanted their ending (future) to be good. He wants our ending to be good.

God made it clear from the beginning that death would be the price for disobedience. Nonetheless, He had already thought of a remedy that would impact our eternity. Though Jesus was the remedy, He would not come to earth for many years. For the sake of Adam and Eve and all those before Christ, God would make the first foreshadowing of the *One to come* by placing coats of skin on Adam and Eve. God clothed them. He covered them with His covering!

The skins that He clothed them with would have to come by the death of an animal. This provision of skins may have been a practical covering, protecting them from the conditions that the world would face as a result of their sin, such as thorns and thistles or weather changes. But more importantly, God was showing them what was required to cover sin now that it had entered the world, and was providing what they needed to approach a Holy God. Adam and Eve's leaf coverings were partial and weak; but God's skin clothing was a head-to-toe covering that wrapped around Adam and Eve *completely.*

Hebrews chapter 10 speaks about the covering of sins through sacrifices which took place before the death of Christ. The animal sacrifices could not actually take away their sins, but only foreshadow the One perfect sacrifice to come. Also, the animal sacrifices were a reminder of sins so that those making the offering did not become numb in conscience. The offerings could not make a person perfect, otherwise they would be offered continually with no intention to stop sinning.

In addition to all that, even the most perfect animal could

not possibly atone for sin. It would take a perfect human for an ultimate sacrifice. It would also take an infinite being to be able to die and conquer death itself. No animal could ever do that.

Instead, one Man would do once and for all what many animal sacrifices could not do a millions times over. Jesus would fulfill the ultimate sacrifice. As Hebrews 10:9b says, "He taketh away the first, that he may establish the second." With Jesus, there would be no more animal sacrifices. No more temporary coverings. Jesus was the *second* and His sacrifice was final.

Jesus offers to clothe us in His robe of righteousness. He offers the complete covering of our sins. This covering was preplanned and pictured all the way back in Genesis. Though man had already been created, God desired to create him again. Sin did not discourage God from wanting a relationship with man. Instead, God carried out his forethought of redemption through Jesus Christ.

Not long after my son was talking pretty well, he started repeating a sentence whenever he had been disobedient. He'd cry and say, "I wanna try again!" He would literally walk back to the spot where he knew his disobedience began. For instance, if it started in the living room by the couch and we were now in another room or another spot within the room, he would go back to the couch where it had begun. He would want me to speak to him like I had before he got in trouble so he could answer me properly and act with obedience the second time around. It was such a complex concept for a small child but it made sense to him. He wanted to try again.

Although we can't exactly replay our life moments, we can begin again in our hearts. After a certain potter in Jeremiah 18 recreates a vessel, the Lord says, "Can I not, O house of Israel, deal with you as this potter does?... "Behold, like the clay in the potter's hand, so are you in My hand" (v.6 NASB).

Do you know what God is saying to you? He's saying, "Let's start again!" As the potter did not want to shatter the vessel into pieces, neither does God want to shatter you. As the potter did not want to discard the vessel in the trash, neither does God want to discard you.

He's saying, "I want to remake you. I want to reshape you; remold you; recreate you; repurpose you; redefine you; revise you; reclaim you. I desire to redeem and restore you!"

If you need a new start, the Potter is offering it. The Potter who created you, preplanned to recreate you! He can make you new (2 Corinthians 5:17). He can form you again in Christ Jesus (Ephesians 2:10).

Go back to the place in your heart where you were disobedient and tell Him that you "wanna try again." Tell Him you want your heart remolded. Agree to get on His Potter's wheel. Once you're on the wheel, stay on it! Put your shoulders down. Relax your body. And enjoy the best massage you'll ever get!

I didn't say that working out the knots would be pain-free, but it's the best because the masseuse is one whose hands produce beauty. As God remolds you, He will say what He said on the sixth day of creation at the beginning of the world: "It is very good."

Alpha, Omega and Jesus

Satan and man have, since the beginning of earthly time, attempted to rule over God and become the Omega (one who cannot be overpowered; the end). Saying it like this sounds silly to those who believe in God, but actually, every time we sin, we are attempting to take over and dethrone Him.

What does it mean that God, as Omega, cannot be overpowered? What makes Him the final authority? How do we know that good will triumph over evil?

There is one good reason we know God and good will always win. There is one good reason that those who lived before Christ knew they were on the winning side. There is one good reason that those of us who live today know He will come back for us and win the final war against Satan. And the reason is—the two who oppose each other are *not* equal forces battling-it-out for the win!

God is Alpha and Creator. Satan is the created. Genesis 3:1a says, "Now the serpent was more subtil than any beast of the field which the LORD God had made." Colossians 1:16 tells us that God created everything, the visible and invisible. There is none who can match the power of God because everything that exists is by His hand.

Even if man for one foolish moment thought that he could overpower God and become the Omega, the end of it all, he clearly must have forgotten that God is also the Alpha. He is the beginning. Man exists simply because God formed and breathed him into existence. Beyond that, the free-will of man exists because a Sovereign God said so. No one besides God will ever be Alpha, and therefore, He will always remain Omega.

Charles Spurgeon in The Metropolitan Tabernacle Pulpit Sermons said this:

> Nay, but O man, who art thou that repliest against God? If he says it, it is so. Believe it. Canst thou not understand it? Who art thou that thou shouldst understand? Canst thou hold the sea in the hollow of thy hand, or

> grasp the winds in thy fist? Worm of the dust, the infinite must ever be beyond thee! There must always be about the glorious Lord somewhat that is incomprehensible, and it is not for thee to doubt because thou canst not understand, but rather humbly to bow before his awful presence who has made thee, and in whose hand thy breath is.[3]

A good reminder of God as Alpha and Creator does not necessarily make us comprehend better, but rather, surrender completely. The Creator has more power and wisdom than His creation—and man's realization of this produces humility.

In struggles of man vs. man, each tries to "out-omega" the other. Whoever wins will just be "out-omega'd" by someone else later on down the road. By comparison, when it comes to God vs. man, there is no competition for who will remain the Omega, because in this case there is an Alpha. Alpha trumps all. Alpha cannot be defeated.

Ever since man has recognized the power of the Alpha, he has begun the attempt to eliminate God as Alpha and Creator. Many have denied the existence of God in order to disclaim Him as Alpha. Others have become resigned to the imaginations of evolution in order to dictate a different beginning. Even some claiming Christ have settled on the collaboration of God and evolution by adding and subtracting from God's Word in order to appease man but still claim heaven.

This is not only wrong, but it also makes God less personal. If He did not breathe into us the breath of life and create us in His own image, then we have made Him out to be an unapproachable God in the sky that we hardly belong to.

If we make Him less personal and diminish His ownership of us, then we don't have to answer to Him. If we can add and remove from the Bible, then truth, right and wrong can hardly be defined. And that is the point: man wants to define his own truth and way. Ultimately, he wants to run his own life.

How does the Redeemer come into all of this? Jesus said, "I am the way, and the truth, and the life" (John 14:6 NASB). Jesus is the only one who can offer us eternal life because He is the only one who could conquer death. Jesus has Omega power. He has Omega power because He has Alpha power. The One who is Alpha and Creator is Omega. Whoever is the beginning, is the winner in the end. **The Beginning, The End.** If you believe Jesus won against Satan (and He did) it's because you know He is Alpha and Omega!

Jesus himself said, "I am Alpha and Omega, the beginning and the end, the first and the last" (Revelation 22:13). And Alpha and Omega declared His love for us on the cross!

He loves us because we are *His*! We are *His* creation, made in *His* image. John 1:1-3 says, "In the beginning was the Word, and the Word was with God, and the Word was God. He was in the beginning with God. All things came into being through Him, and apart from Him nothing came into being that has come into being" (NASB). The Creator and Jesus are *one*. They go together. They exist in unison. They preplanned redemption together!

My five-year-old boy, JJ, is about the most precious earthly gift God has given me. He was prayed for long before he was born. I'm sure I must kiss him one hundred or more times a day. And each day I find myself saying to him, "Do you know why I love you so much? It's because you're Mama's baby."

We are HIS baby! Don't you know that God created man

with a plan of redemption long before Adam and Eve ever sinned? Don't you know that He has gone great lengths to bring you back to Himself? Don't you know that He loves you?

If He wasn't Creator, if He wasn't Alpha, if you weren't His, then a buy-back plan would have never been purchased. Jesus would not have gone through all that He did—nor would He have the power to accomplish it.

But He *could* and He *did*—because *HE IS.* He overpowered death and the grave and He will overcome Satan in the end because He existed before anyone else and He created all that exists. He is sovereign and He held the supremacy long before time on earth began!

Before the dive into Genesis 4 (about the life of Cain and Abel), believe in the God of Genesis 1, 2, and 3. For He is declaring to you, "I AM Creator, I AM Alpha and Omega—and you, my creation, I have come to redeem!"

As we move into Genesis 4 and look into the lives of Cain and Abel, note that we will follow the account in order as it is written in God's Word. In this book, the beginning of each chapter includes the verses that will be covered in order to provide clarity and understanding for the next many pages.

Let's continue the identity journey as we take a deep look into the hearts of the world's first two brothers!

Chapter 2

Raising Cain and Abel

My Shepherd, My Direction

And Adam knew Eve his wife; and she conceived, and bare Cain, and said, I have gotten a man from the LORD. And she again bare his brother Abel. And Abel was a keeper of sheep, but Cain was a tiller of the ground. (Genesis 4:1-2)

My son, observe the commandment of your father And do not forsake the teaching of your mother; Bind them continually on your heart; Tie them around your neck. When you walk about, they will guide you; When you sleep, they will watch over you; And when you awake, they will talk to you. For the commandment is a lamp and the teaching is light; And reproofs for discipline are the way of life. (Proverbs 6:20-23 NASB)

Birth Order

After the fall and consequences of Adam and Eve in Genesis 3, these first parents picked up some obedience in Chapter 4. God had told them to be fruitful and multiply—and they did. More beginnings were to come, including the first birth.

It's hard to imagine being Eve at this point. Not only were there no doctors, hospitals or even scissors to cut the umbilical cord, but through her own knowledge, Eve may not have known that there would be an umbilical cord. There were no books telling her what to expect.

Cain was the firstborn child. Adam and Eve must have been delighted. After Cain, Abel was born. There is probability that these two may have been twins. Despite the fact that other siblings would be born after them but before their brother Seth, the only names listed for us are Cain and Abel. They may have been the only two males at the time.

At the birth of Cain, Eve said, "I have gotten a man from the LORD" (Genesis 4:1). This statement can likely indicate that she had the child with the Lord's help. If this is so, we can certainly see why. She needed His help to get through all the unknowns of the first delivery.

However, some scholars suggest that Eve's comment had more to do with her thinking that Cain was the promised seed that was spoken of by the Lord when He said to the serpent (Satan), "I will put enmity between thee and the woman, and between thy seed and her seed; it shall bruise thy head, and thou shalt bruise his heel" (Genesis 3:15).

This verse is a sure sign of the gospel of Jesus Christ and how He will defeat Satan. His heel may be stricken on the cross but He will crush Satan's head by His triumph over the grave and later bind him for all eternity.

Adam and Eve's possible presumptions may have set the wrong tone for raising Cain and Abel. Did Eve think

Cain was the *promised* seed? Did she rely on her own understanding of the Lord's redemption plan? If so, her thoughts couldn't have lasted very long. By the time her kids hit the "terrible two's" Eve must have realized she was raising stolen identities. She must have known she was raising children with a sin nature.

Notice there is no record of Eve commenting after the birth of Abel. Did she put all her hope in Cain as the *first* seed? Did these new parents place much emphasis on the firstborn child?

A reading of the Bible reveals that certain rights and privileges had been placed on the firstborn male. The firstborn son would inherit his father's estate. The firstborn had the right to one day attain what his father owned. This gain would come with a responsibility and as well as a position of leadership. The firstborn was the "lord" over his siblings. He was in a position to lead, direct and instruct. He was in the position of commander under the guidance and rule of his father.

As Cain carried out his firstborn rights, did he forget that there was a commander over him? Two commanders (both his father and God) over him? Cain was not just the firstborn of Adam and Eve but the firstborn son of the world! Did he believe that he was "Lord" of all creation?

Colossians 1:15b tells us that Jesus is the "the firstborn of all creation" (NASB). This means that He is Lord of it. Verse 18b says of Jesus, "who is the beginning, the firstborn from the dead; that in all *things* he might have the preeminence." This means that He was first in time, He was the first to rise again and He should hold first place in our hearts.

Perhaps Cain took his firstborn rights too far. Perhaps he failed in leadership because he refused to have Lordship over him! Perhaps he wanted first place. The highest seat. The adoration.

For these reasons, the firstborn child does not always secure the firstborn's title or birthright. History has revealed times where God has used the second born, a younger child, or even the youngest child to obtain the birthright or higher position.

Remember Jacob and Esau? Esau was the oldest son that the Lord said would come to serve his younger brother. Like Cain, he was a man of the field, but instead of tilling the ground for fruit, he was a hunter. For by this time in history, meat had become a food option. Later in the story, Esau sold his birthright to Jacob in exchange for food.

Then there is Joseph, son of Jacob. Like the accounts of Cain and Esau, this too is another story of jealousy. Joseph's older brothers sold him into slavery while manipulating their father to believe he had died from an animal attack. God used the wickedness of his brothers to lead Joseph on a journey that would take him to a top position in Egypt. Later on, his brothers were forced to bow before him and beg for mercy.

Lastly, there's no forgetting David, the shepherd boy who had a heart for God. While his older brothers lined up for Samuel the prophet in hopes that they would be picked as the next king, David was in the field carrying out his daily responsibilities. Samuel passed by each son of Jesse as none of them were the one of which God had spoken. It was the youngest one; the shepherd boy in the field that God was calling. God made David *firstborn* (Psalms 89:27).

I do wonder how Cain grew up. Did Adam and Eve place much on his shoulders as firstborn? Were the expectations of Cain so high that he always felt the need to impress his parents? Did Cain grow up with a mindset of a false identity of who he was supposed to become?

Certainly, Adam and Eve must have told the children *their* story. They must have told them about their sin and the price of that sin: death. Perhaps Eve's delight in the birth of Cain had less to do with her thinking he would be the redeeming seed and more to do with her delight that humankind would not be wiped out; that human life would continue even if physical death would eventually occur.

Certainly, Adam and Eve must have also told their children about God's declaration to redeem humankind. And upon hearing it, maybe then it was actually Cain who wanted himself to be the redeeming seed. Maybe it was he that imagined being firstborn, not just of Adam and Eve, but of all. Perhaps he had puffed up his own image with a pride that desired power. Potentially the expectations and demands of being the superhero firstborn seed came from within.

Cain

The name Cain means "To produce, beget, acquire."[4] Perhaps his producing and acquiring began in childhood. Before growing up and having an occupation that would relate to his name meaning, what kinds of things might Cain have sought to produce or acquire at an early age?

Did Cain want his parents to be more proud of him than Abel? Did he use manipulative words for profit? Did he play one parent verses the other to achieve his desires? By producing his own independence, did he refuse help from others because he believed his wisdom and expertise superseded the need for intervention? Did he want his siblings to use him and his talents as a measuring stick of what they should live up to? Was he obsessed with gaining approval, to know that he was the best, smartest, fastest, handsomest, strongest, funniest, most skillful, most creative kid on the block? Perhaps even the most seemingly spiritual?

You see, I wonder if Cain was the kind of kid that was

unsatisfied from youth—and if so, did anyone try to do anything about it? I wonder if what should have been "little blessings from above" were never good enough for him. Was his idea of what he wanted to obtain so grand that the little things in life had no effect on him?

I wonder how he interacted with Abel. Did he endlessly seek to compete with his brother to gain a win? Was he so insecure with his identity that he had to attempt to control his brother's identity?

When Cain's "little" brother attempted to learn a new skill (such as riding a bike in today's time) that Cain had already mastered, did Cain use his firstborn leadership to display the character of patience? Did he cheer with excitement as his brother got better at the skill? Or did he speak degrading words like, "You're not doing that right! You'll never get it! You don't know anything. Give it to me!"? Did he feel the need to show off how much better he was than Abel?

Why consider so many questions and propositions about Cain's childhood? We should consider them because Cain's wicked *ending* points to an unresolved problem at his *beginning*! Ecclesiastes 10:13 says, "the beginning of his talking is folly and the end of it is wicked madness" (NASB). Cain was born in sin and his ending confirms that he remained in it. What happened during the years in between was all the building up of what was revealed at his end. His childhood led to adulthood. Pride occurred before destruction (Proverbs 16:18).

To question Cain's possible motives from birth will give us some insight into our own lives. It will help us analyze how character builds up over time; how one poor choice leads to another poor choice. Looking at Cain's probable path, from first breath to final destruction, gives us opportunity to change our own path before it ends.

> **The point of dissecting Cain's heart and actions will be to help us *recognize* and *overcome* the "Cain" within *us* and to help our children *recognize* and *overcome* the "Cain" within *them*. This will lead us both to become our own unique "Abel."**

What kinds of possible producing and acquiring issues in Cain can we relate to? What can we see in our children that portrays their love of worldly gain over God? We know producing and acquiring by itself is not the problem—just as money is not. 1 Timothy 6:10 reminds us, "For the love of money is the root of all sorts of evil, and some by longing for it have wandered away from the faith and pierced themselves with many griefs" (NASB). The problem begins in our hearts. And it can develop at a young age.

Regardless of when the problems began in Cain, the desire to produce and acquire was evident in his adulthood. Genesis records that Cain was a tiller of the ground. Adam was also a tiller and Cain, being the firstborn, followed in his father's footsteps.

Cain's job was to farm and till the land for produce that would be nourishment for him and his family. This task would be necessary, but it sure wouldn't be easy. For God declared in Genesis 3 that the ground would be cursed (v.17), that there would be thorns and thistles (v.18) and that it would be hard, sweaty work (v.19) until they died and returned to that very ground. Both Adam and Cain had some tough days ahead of them.

The connection of the meaning of Cain's name and his occupation are too strong to be coincidence. To *acquire* land and *produce* on it, even in our day, is a prize and possession that many long for and seek to achieve. There is nothing on earth that is more real, lasting and tangible than property.

Ecclesiastes 1:4 says, "One generation goes, one generation comes, but the land lasts forever."

If Cain chose his occupation, then he chose the one that was lasting; the one that wouldn't go out of business; the one that was stable; the one that would always be needed. Now, in many ways, this seems pretty wise of him. But based on Cain's revealing character in later verses, I wonder if other intentions were really behind it.

Did Cain choose the *tiller* occupation out of greed? Did he choose it to impress his father, who also had that occupation? Or maybe it was to be close to his father in order to feel needed and important? Was it to be able to brag to other siblings or family members that he had all the inside scoop with a level of control on how the family business was carried out? Did he choose it in hopes to secure and establish his rights as firstborn because he did not rest in God alone?

What if Cain had the option of becoming a shepherd to care for the creatures that would be devoted and sacrificed to the Lord? What if he passed up that right to Abel because he had no interest in God, found the position boring or simply wanted more fame instead of the solitude shepherding would bring?

Quite possibly he didn't make any choice at all, but simply found himself in the position which was given to him. Potentially, he could have turned this position into a blessing and learning experience, but instead he became prideful within.

Could Cain not have seen all the parallels between his job and his heart? Did he observe weeds choking out a plant, or a tree that became uprooted, and not equate them to spiritual matters? Did he prune his garden and somehow miss the connection of God doing a work in him? As he planted new seeds, which would later produce a good harvest, was the message of spiritual reaping and sowing so unfamiliar? Perhaps, over time, Cain began to block out all the evidences of God.

His choice or not, Cain became a tiller of land. Much of the reason that land is a prize is because it is a place. It's a place to call home. It's where we find comfort, stability and love. We lay down our roots in a place, marry, have children, and make memories.

How ever old Cain was at the time of the offerings, we can likely conclude that he is already married based on the later half of Genesis chapter four. Cain is not a child anymore. He is well grounded with his land, occupation, wife and immediate family.

Family Living

In 1987 my father scoped out a plot of land on the West Side of Syracuse. I'm told by my mother that my dad walked every inch of that land over and over. He knew every dip, every tree and each square foot. He studied it, memorized it and finally started making plans to build on it. It was an overgrown lot with trees, weeds, rocks and a steep hill in the back that led to the woods and a creek known as Harbor Brook. Somehow, as my dad footed the space, he saw potential. He saw a home. He saw *his* home.

I was a five-year-old girl but I can still close my eyes and see movie clips while the house was being built. It's my two uncles, my father's brothers, laying the foundation. It's the feeling of fear as I climb up a ladder to see the second level of the house because the stairs hadn't been built yet. And it's the smell of a small potted tree on the very first Christmas in an unfinished house.

As time went on, other memories were formed. My brother and I would often cross that creek to explore land on the other side or walk the creek upstream to meet up with our only neighbors who had kids our age. Other days were filled with costumes and acting in our theater (a.k.a. our back deck) with kids my mother would babysit during the summer.

My mother was a crafter, a cook, and no doubt a dreamer. She was our teacher during our homeschool years and founder of a small Christian school during the later half of our schooling days. Baking was her specialty and still is, as my parents now own a local bakery and café.

In my dad's world (outside of his office job), days were filled with inventing, fixing the next problem on a vehicle or getting after the "dumb mutt' as he often said. Those who know my dad know he has a unique ability to invent things especially if it could save him a buck or two. There was no exception when it came to tilling the ground on the new land.

To avoid renting a rototiller, my dad decided to rig up his ancient and rickety tractor. He hooked up a heavy duty rake to the back of it and placed cinder blocks on top to weigh it down—and off he drove. I have no idea how it all worked, but somehow he made it happen.

These are the roots of my family, and to prove my point one step further, the roots are so deep within me that I cannot seem to leave this house and land. It's personal. It's the house my father built. The land he once walked and continues to walk. And so, we all live here... under one roof!

I can only imagine what it must have been like to live in the first days of the earth. Adam and Eve must have lived close to, if not with, their adult children. They must have discovered the world together and done some inventing as well. They must have built memories and roots as the first family. They must have worked together to accomplish good living.

After all, Abel needed to eat of the fruit that Cain produced from tilling the ground and Cain needed to wear the clothes that would be made from the sheep that Abel kept. I wonder if all this was a family business.

Abel

Second born is Abel. His name means "breath, vanity."[5] Some have described his name as the visible breath which pours out of one's mouth on a bitter winter day. You see it for a second and then it disappears. It bears the same idea as the word *vanity* in Ecclesiastes. Later, in the New Testament, we are reminded that our life is but a vapor or breath (James 4:14).

The connection between Abel's name and his life also seem too strong for coincidence. It is hard to know if Eve named her children or if the Lord did. The passage does not give us that information but interestingly enough, it does later state that Eve is the one who names her younger son, Seth. If Eve also named Abel, it could have been because she realized that the life span of humankind is as a breath (Psalm 39:5). If it was the Lord who named him, it may have been because He knew his life would be short.

Abel was, by occupation, a keeper of sheep. Abel's job as shepherd could not have been easy either. On the surface, it may seem like he got a simple or even lazy job. I mean, all he had to do was sit around and watch a bunch of slow and boring sheep, right?

Telling a shepherd that he has an easy job is like telling a mother that she has an easy job. There is much more to *tending* and *caring* than often meets the eye! We also know that God is the good shepherd who "lays down His life for the sheep" (John 10:11 NASB). Shepherding requires leadership, sacrifice, compassion, patience, strong character and an abundance of love!

Sheep and goats were most likely kept at this early stage in the world for three main reasons. One: sheep may have been kept for milk or cheese. If this is true, perhaps it had become a bit threatening to Cain that he wasn't the only one who contributed to the food business.

Two: they were kept for fabric to make clothing. God was the originator of this, as Adam and Eve, after sinning, knew that they were naked. It was God who clothed them with skins (Genesis 3:21).

Three: sheep may have been kept for sacrifice. As God clothed Adam and Eve with the skins, blood must have been shed to obtain those skins. This is but a glimpse of the first sacrifice for sin and certainly we will see more of that through Abel.

As the sheep were bred, plans may have been orchestrated to set aside the firstborn, spotless or most valuable ones to later use as a sin offering to the Lord.

If Abel chose the shepherd occupation, it is likely that he did care for God's creation as well as what would be devoted to his Lord. I can only imagine that his daily responsibilities were carried out with utmost attention, quality and detail.

I wonder if Abel was a type of David. In his solitude in the fields, did he sing out praises unto the Lord? Did he commune with God and listen for His voice? Did he pour out his heart by letting go of the cares and worries of the world? Did he view the hills, trees and sky in awe and wonder of the Lord's handiwork? Did his heart find contentment, peace and true joy because he was secure in who God was, who he was and what the Lord had called him to do?

I wonder what he was like as a child. Did he always have a heart that desired the things of the Lord? Did he develop tenderness toward spiritual matters? Did he listen to his father's and mother's instructions and hide them in his heart? Did he learn from their previous poor choices? Did he recognize the devil's schemes and stand against them? Surely he wasn't perfect. So, what were his struggles and weaknesses and what did he go through to overcome them? What kind of heart-wrestling took place as he grew up?

No matter how Abel was raised, he *chose* faith. No matter what sins he had committed, he *chose* to surrender.

Raising our Sheep

We are not entirely sure how Cain and Abel grew up. We can't be confident about what occurred between the time of their birth and the time they became established in their occupations. An obvious span of time took place in just the first two verses of Genesis 4.

What we do know is that although Adam and Eve acted as shepherds to Cain and Abel, these first children needed to choose in their hearts whether or not they were going to follow their shepherds, learn from their shepherds and heed advice from their shepherds.

As we shepherd our own children, we need to consider how we can best lead them, teach them and reach them. I am not a counselor or doctor of any kind. But over the years, I have taken note of how I was raised and how others raised their children. I've taken note of the good and the bad and here is a list of helpful tips I've come up with that I strongly believe in.

On a side note, I am still amazed at my parents' abilities to raise us kids as well as so many other kids that they took under their wings over the years. I also admit that I am still learning many things myself as I parent my own child.

1. **Joy or Misery** - A disobedient child is an unhappy one—and this is especially easy to see when the child is young. In a battle of you vs. your child, the longer they refuse to obey, the more miserable they become. Attitudes, whining, complaints and words like "No" are expressed. This often leads to anger, tears or an outright temper tantrum. Certainly, they are anything but happy.

A child who is obedient is generally happy and pleasant. There are few or no battles and storms occurring in their heart, and therefore they act appropriately with attitudes of compliance. They are joyful in spirit, which is one of several rewards that corresponds to their obedience.

No child will ever be perfect, since we are all born with a sin nature. However, understanding this concept will help parents reevaluate what is going on with their child as they face the many ups, downs and stages of their child's life.

As we get older, the only thing that changes is that we learn how to manipulate in a smarter capacity. We learn that we can disobey God and pretend to others and even ourselves that life is just dandy. It is true that sin can be pleasurable for a time but that is short-lived. Eventually, sin becomes sickening, hollow and flat-out miserable. Cain's misery will prove his disobedience.

There is something about obedience that gives us true joy. Not just feelings of goodness in our hearts, but a washing that cleanses our souls and makes us joyful in the Lord. We are truly happiest when we are right with God and are following after His will and way. Obedience makes us joyful and Abel will prove this point.

Psalms 119:1 says, "How blessed are those whose way is blameless, who walk in the law of the LORD" (NASB).

2. **Wisdom** - Our children need instructions and sound teaching. They need us to pass on to them a love for

God's Word. They need to be told that there is life in God's commandments. They need a shepherd to tell them what is important to acquire.

Proverbs 4:5a says, "Acquire wisdom! Acquire understanding!" (NASB). Why? Because wisdom is a guard against foolishness. Wisdom is a keeper against evil. Wisdom is a giver of benefits. Wisdom makes us conquerors. Wisdom honors us. Wisdom takes us down a path that is straight, lit and balanced (Proverbs 4).

We can teach our children particular skills. We can teach them to be resourceful. We can give them the best education. We can even prod them to advance their talents. But it all proves vain if we don't teach them to gain wisdom from God. It all proves empty if we don't shepherd their heart in the right direction.

The proof that our children love knowledge and wisdom is if they have a willingness to be taught (Proverbs 12:1). They cannot be allowed to command a teacher position as if they know everything. Rather, they must recognize their position as a student who is eager to learn. They need to have a willingness to be guided by the shepherd. This is true for all of us when it comes to our relationship with God.

3. **Direction** – We need to teach our children to look down the road. We need to show them how each step is taking them in a particular direction. The direction they walk in has consequences or rewards; lies or truth; death or life. If they look down the path, they can see where their contemplated steps will lead.

God's Word tells us *what* steps lead *where*. This is why Psalms 119:105 says, "Your word is a lamp to my feet and a light to my path" (NASB). His Word shines a light so that our steps can be established.

4. **Access and Supervision** - Children have been given "too much access with too little supervision". This is something I started saying just a couple of years ago as I've observed children and teens with devices of many kinds without any boundaries, parental controls, etc. Children have been given *access to too much.*

Not only is there too much access but there is little or no *supervision.* Parents are often unaware when a sin problem arises in their child's life—a problem caused by their child having too much access! Parents sometimes avoid engaging with their children unless a major catastrophe bursts forth that they're forced to pay attention to.

If you combine *too much access* with *too little supervision,* you come out with a child who can do anything they want. And that "anything" is bent toward the sin nature. What we end up with is children who are naughty and miserable, and not long after we ask, "how did they get this way?"

Cut back on the access and engage in the little lives who need real shepherding.

Proverbs 29:15 says "The rod and reproof give wisdom: but a child left to *himself* bringeth his mother to shame."

5. **Thank you and I'm sorry** - Teaching children to say these statements is easy and enforced by most parents when children are first learning to speak and during preschool or early childhood age. It is mostly taught that it is the polite thing to do—and it is. Sometime later on down the road as the child grows into middle school or pre-teen age, this principle gets lost. Children lose some of that young innocence and realize that "thank you" and "I'm sorry" often become a bit more of a humbling experience.

Looking back, as a child there was nothing tougher than being forced to call someone (especially an adult) and say "I'm sorry," but my mother made us. Even if I was truly sorry in my heart, to actually have to say it humbled me more than I can explain.

The same is true for "thank you." I've met more children that are ungrateful than I wish to have. Teaching your children to write "thank you notes" or say "thank you" on the spot is beyond valuable. Teaching them *what* to be thankful for is immeasurable.

It is one thing to be thankful for the card and money you received for a birthday and it's another to be thankful for the time, work and example of someone special in your life. In prayer, it's the difference between "thank you for all that You have given me" and "thank you, God, for all that You are." All of these "thank you's" are good and appropriate but the second goes deeper. Teach your children to have a "thank you" heart whose depth goes beyond tangibles.

6. **Your Authority** - When children do become disobedient, the idea is to get them to recognize and confess their sin and to get them back on the right path. When the child continues to battle and fight for their own way, the parent must *emphatically,* sometimes with *creativity* and often through *longevity,* take the win. It can be easy to back down, especially if the battle seems to continue on and on without an end in sight. Don't do it. Continue to enforce the right way no matter how many times it takes for the child to submit. If you don't come out a winner, your child will. This will set the tone for who is in charge for all the years to come.

7. **Key Phrases** - Especially when children are younger and can only understand a limited amount of language, it is important to repeat key phrases to them over and over. It can be the simplest phrases like, "Jesus loves you," "God

made you," "You're mama's baby" and "It's much happier to be obedient."

Throughout their lives, we need to speak words of identity. Speak phrases that tell your child who God is and who they are. It's vital that children know the truth from the beginning. Speak godly phrases that resonate in their mind.

Hebrew 8:10 says, "For this *is* the covenant that I will make with the house of Israel after those days, saith the Lord; I will put my laws into their mind, and write them in their hearts: and I will be to them a God, and they shall be to me a people." Fill their mind and heart with good from the start.

8. **Identity Issues** - As precious as our children are, they are born with an overall sin nature as well as specific sin tendencies and weaknesses. Even at a young age, a child's individual beliefs about his/her identity is evident in the specific sin issues with which he/she struggles.

As your child grows, learn what he or she struggles with most. Talk about it with them, give discipline to it early on and learn how to help them overcome it. Over the years, their particular struggle may change or come out in various forms because of a new stage of life. Knowing the core of those issues will help you stay ahead of the game, understand what to look for when you suspect something is not right with your child and move forward with specific scriptures that will help your child combat that problem.

Remember—we need to help our children *recognize* and *overcome* the "Cain" within them!

9. **Value** - Teach your children the value of people, property and possessions. You can achieve this by setting the example. Show love, concern and interest for others when they are sick, in need and even when exciting events

take place in their lives. This will show your children that you care about others tribulations and that you support their triumph's without jealousy.

For property and possessions, take care of them in a way that declares their value. Society has pushed for the quantity of items that are disposable. Less tangibles of higher quality that are cared for, promote their value as well as develop responsibility from the owner.

All of this teaches children that people, property and possessions are not dispensable. They have worth and should be treated as such.

10. **Shame and Mercy** - If there's sin, let the moment be shameful. I like to say, "Let it be what it is." Be careful not to be so quick at covering the shame that there practically is none. Children need to know that sin is wrong, unacceptable and shameful. Let them feel that. Tears may be necessary. Be ready for and offer the mercy covering of sin, but let them desire that covering through the admission that they need it. They need to be sorry for their disobedience. If you do this, it will make the mercy act all the more joyful and their hearts all the more authentic!

11. **Love** - No matter what your child has done, at the end of the day, tell them you love them. Tomorrow will start a fresh day to live, but tonight they need to be held and loved. Tonight they need security and assurance that they are still your baby.

12. **Prayer** - After your child has fallen asleep (or anytime, really), simply place your hand on their heart and thank God for creating them, praise Jesus for dying for them and ask for the Holy Spirit to bring conviction to your child. Pour your heart out before the Lord and then entrust your

child into the hands of the only God who can do a work in them!

Again, I am not an expert. At times I struggle with what to do just like every other parent. I am learning and growing and understanding more and more as I go. What I do know for certain is, I will have to answer for what I did with the responsibility God has so graciously given me: shepherding a child.

I want to raise my boy to become more like Abel and less like Cain, but complete in Jesus! I want to know that I used all my efforts of love, forgiveness, sacrifice and shepherding while raising the life that God has entrusted to me. I want to know that I, (both by example and word) led my sheep to the Good Shepherd.

Ultimately, each person can only answer for themselves. You cannot force anyone, even your own child, into following his or her Creator. But what you can do and are responsible to do is to raise them in a way that will help shape them toward their true identity; the identity God designed for them long ago (Ephesians 2:10).

As for Cain and Abel, their character began to develop during their childhood. Cain's disobedience to God may have been evident by his disobedience to his parents at an early age. I'm not sure how well he kept the 5th commandment of honoring his parents (at least in his heart) if he refused to obey the 1st commandment of having no other gods. At minimum, he refused the spiritual shepherding of his parents who were likely steering him to the Shepherd of the universe!

Ultimately each sin of every heart leads back to the root of not allowing God to rule and reign within us. We need to let Him have first place in our hearts! We need the powerful hands of the One who will pluck our wicked root as well as grow a new glorious garden within us. We need the mighty rod and tender staff of the Shepherd who can fight off the wolf and carry us back to the fold.

Without a shepherd, we wander in the way of uncertainty. With a shepherd, we're settled on the path of assurance. The Good Shepherd leads us in the right way! If we choose to follow His preeminent leading, we automatically choose which direction we are headed. **My Shepherd, My Direction.**

Chapter 3

The Offerings

My Faith: Past and Future, My Faith: Present

And in the process of time it came to pass, that Cain brought of the fruit of the ground an offering unto the LORD. And Abel, he also brought of the firstlings of his flock and of the fat thereof. And the LORD had respect unto Abel and to his offering: But unto Cain and to his offering he had not respect. (Genesis 4:3-5a)

By faith Abel offered unto God a more excellent sacrifice than Cain. (Hebrews 11:4a)

Let the words of my mouth and the meditation of my heart Be acceptable in Your sight, O LORD, my rock and my Redeemer. (Psalm 19:14)

As Cain and Abel grew up, they became established in their occupations. As time progressed, they each brought an offering to the Lord. It seems likely that this may have been Cain and Abel's first offering as adults.

As we look at the offerings of Cain and Abel, several questions begin to surface. Why was Cain's offering rejected? Was it because of what he brought, his heart, or a combination of both? Why was Abel's offering respected? How did he know what would be favorable?

For clarification about the word "respect," this is the same word as "regard." Regard is the Hebrew word *Shaah* and means "to gaze."[6] It means to consider, look with favor on or behold. It also has the idea of inspecting or examining. It's like a newborn baby that is both desirable to gaze on and irresistible to not survey head to toe.

God had regard for one of two offerings. He had regard for one of two men. Let's decipher the offerings and examine why.

There are several factors to consider that will help us understand the offerings better, including the **excellence**, **type**, **ownership** and **heart** of them. The New Testament will also give insightful information about the brothers themselves.

Below is an analysis of *what* they each brought.

Cain: brought of *the* fruit of *the* ground *an* offering (v.3; emphasis added).

Abel: brought of the *firstlings* of *his* flock and of the *fat* thereof (v.4; emphasis added).

Excellence

By dissecting the verses describing the offerings, it

becomes immediately clear that Abel's offering reflects words of description and value. As we look at Cain's offering, we can tell that a certain quality and **excellence** is lacking. What grade of fruit was it? What condition was it in? What was the worth or value of it?

Ever been apple picking? There is much more to the great state of New York than just New York City. Don't get me wrong, the city is a great place to visit (especially for me, since my brother lives there) but New York is also apple country and fall can only be as beautiful in just a few other states. Every October, my mom and I drive twenty-five short minutes to Lafayette for apple picking at Deer Run Farms. The crisp, fresh air, the vibrant colors of the trees and the morning sun causing elongated shadows make for a much needed and refreshing time.

We get our bags to collect our apples in and head out to the rows of trees from which we desire to pick. Even if it's not previously on my brain whatsoever, I am instantly hit with thoughts of Adam and Eve. Though an apple may not have been the fruit that played a part in the fall of man, it's almost difficult to avoid thoughts of their story and the beginning of time.

Existing on the sinful side of the fall of man makes me long to taste the apples that were once unaffected by the curse. Adam and Eve are the only two who had that opportunity and were later forced to work harder as well as eat a less desirable fruit.

Can you imagine perfect apple trees with perfect fruit on them? Oh, how delectably crisp and sweet they must have been!

As I continue walking down the rows of trees, I have to examine every apple before I pick it. These are not perfect, "garden of Eden" type apples after all. Some are not ripe.

Some have worm holes and yet others are rotten. I look down at the fallen ones that lay on the ground and I ask myself silly questions like, "Why did they fall? Were they overripe? Did a wind gust come through? Did they get knocked off the tree while someone was reaching for another apple? Did they just get dropped?"

Over the last couple years, my mind has added the thoughts of Cain on to our apple picking adventures. What kind of fruit did Cain present to the Lord? Was it fallen fruit? Was it all the leftovers, the rotten ones that weren't of any use? Maybe, rather, the fruit was premature. Picked before ripened. Perhaps his offering didn't consist of apples or even other fruits that fell from trees, but maybe it consisted of produce that did not grow well. The fruit may have been small, misshapen or bug infested. These poor quality ones may have lined the bottom two-thirds of some early-world type bowl while fresh produce topped it off, making Cain still look good to others.

Whatever it was, it seems Cain's offering attempted to cheat God out of a certain quality. Our actions are simply an indicator of our heart (Prov. 23:7). We give enough to God in hopes to get us by or in hopes that He will continue to bless us or not punish us. Somehow we think that we can actually fool Him. We think we can buy Him out with our half-quality gifts. We forget that He is not looking for our gifts but our fully devoted hearts. He wants our surrender.

From 2005-2011, I worked for a sporting goods retail company. After a few years of working as a Lead Cashier, I was promoted to the position of Operations Manager. This put me into a unique position within the store. The in-store Asset Protection Agent, a Christian man from Trinidad, called me the "thumb of the store." You see, there were five managers and I was the one with the odd position because my job intertwined with everyone else's job.

The employees called me the "mom" of the store because I took care of everyone as well as any issues that arose (not to mention the food and baked goods I'd bring in). My main responsibilities included how the store operated and functioned in regard to rules and policies, interacting with Human Resources and Asset Protection, managing employees, paperwork of all kinds and oh yes—those dreaded audits.

Over the years, one topic I had to encounter and deal with was employee theft. It happens more often than you would think and after a while I began to expect it. I developed a keen, observational eye that detected and analyzed behaviors of all sorts. If something was missing, I could easily narrow it down to the *who* and the *why*.

After my suspicions were confirmed, either by camera, another witness, or just a narrowing down of "it pretty much has to be," the employee would be interviewed by AP with me as a witness. After the employee admitted to the theft, it was then asked him or her, "Why? Why did you do it? Don't you have a good job here?" To which the answers varied from things like, "I don't know," "Because I could," "I just wanted to," "I thought it would be cool to own [it]," "So and so pressured me" and "I was just bored and had nothing better to do," with a tag line of, "I didn't think it was a big deal." There were many times an underlying attitude that catered to how much money the company had and how it could afford to lose an item here and there and, even more so, how the employee deserved it.

You would be surprised how many of them didn't really need the item they took, nor were they lacking money. Oh, but that "boredom" syndrome—it plagues so many. If you are bored, then you are certainly not doing God's will.

Boredom allows our minds to wander and heart and actions to follow. Before we know it, we are no longer bored but busy doing evil.

And oh, that "deserving" syndrome—it snags so many. The "you have too much and I deserve more" lifestyle won't get you far. It certainly can lead one to taking what is not theirs to begin with—from a piece of gum, to time off the clock, to robbing a bank and even to taking a life!

Could Cain have been bored? Did he lack communion with God, which caused that boredom in the first place? What was his excuse for stealing the quality of his offering from God? Was it, "God, You own everything. Surely you can let me have the quality of my own labor"?

We also find some insight on **excellence** in the New Testament in John 12. Mary (sister of Martha and Lazarus) offered up an expensive ointment over Jesus' feet and wiped them with her hair. Judas questioned why the ointment was not sold and given to the poor. He said this because he was greedy for money. He was a thief about to betray Jesus (John 12:6).

I wonder if Cain was like Judas. When Abel presented his offering, did Cain think it was ridiculous to waste such good sheep and clothing on it? Did Cain, like Judas, attempt to spiritualize his reasons why his offering lacked excellence? Did his quality lacking fruit come with excuses of how the better fruit should be used? Did he secretly have intentions of hoarding or stealing the best for himself?

A previous story of Mary relates her sitting down at Jesus' feet, listening to His teaching. She soaked in His offering and was later able to give Him a precious ointment offering.

When we soak in Jesus, we too are able to give a precious offering. What is inside us will certainly come out. If we are not filled with God, then we are filled with ourselves. A *self* offering will never be accepted. Fill up on Jesus first! Then give Him your heart; your surrender; your best.

Abel's offering was top-grade. The sheep were either firstborn or the best of his flock which declared their *value*. They were either large or plump which declared their *substance*. Seemingly Abel held nothing back from his offering. In fact, Hebrews 11:4 tells us that Abel offered "a more excellent sacrifice."

Did Cain's offering lack quality? Likely. Did Abel's offering possess excellence? Completely!

Type

In addition to not bringing God his best, Cain may have totally disregarded the **type** of offering that should have been brought.

Though we do not have any details of what type of offering should have been brought, we should not assume that none were given. Since day six of creation, we see God giving clear instruction to man. He specifically points out the one tree that should not be eaten from and the consequences should that happen.

From the beginning, God has shown that He is personal. He didn't just create man and drop him off into a garden and say, "Good luck figuring everything out." Instead, He is there directing, informing and desiring the very best for His creation that He made in His image.

God's Word does not state what kind of offering Cain and Abel were supposed to present. We do not know if they were to bring the requirements for a sin offering, a praise offering or another kind of offering.

If it had been a sin offering, Cain and his offering were

not accepted (in part) because he did not bring an animal for sacrifice. Blood was needed and required for sin.

If Cain should have brought a blood sacrifice and didn't, it was probably because in his pride, he did not want to admit he had sin to confess. Perhaps he did not mind bringing a praise offering because he thought it might keep the peace. Or maybe he did not mind thanking God for helping him and his father grow a good crop. But no way was he going to humble or surrender himself.

There is also the possibility that Cain did not want to slaughter a sheep but instead wanted to put on a display of the "fruits" of his own personal labor. Perhaps he could have swapped some of his crops for one of Abel's sheep but instead wanted his work and occupation to be recognized by God as well as others.

Have you ever been given a gift that you had zero interest in but the giver had every interest in? Perhaps the person took no care to think about what *you* liked but only what *they* liked. It almost seems like Cain's type of offering could have been wrong because he did not consider what would please God. Perhaps he looked at his own interests and gave the thing with which he was so obsessed. Again, we do not know what kind of offering this should have been, but we do know the kind of offering, from the kind of person, that was accepted—and blood just so happened to be a part of Abel's offering.

We also know that disobedience will produce a poor sacrifice. This is why the Bible says that God desires obedience more than sacrifice (1 Samuel 15:22). You cannot bring a good sacrifice without obedience and you cannot be obedient without surrender.

After becoming king of Israel, Saul proved this to be true. In 1 Samuel 15, Samuel, the last judge, received word from the Lord in a message which he relayed to Saul. The instructions were to wipe out the Amalekites for their wickedness. The details included killing every Amalekite of every age and gender as well as all the livestock and animals of every kind. Saul was told to keep nothing alive. This task was simple and straightforward and somehow, through sin, Saul complicated it. Instead of doing what the Lord commanded, he killed all the people except king Agag and also kept the best sheep and other good livestock alive.

I want to say, "How is this possible? Your instructions were so direct. How could you mess this up?" In the narration, Samuel approached Saul the next day and questioned the reason for his disobedience. Saul responded that the *people* kept the best of the animals to use as a *sacrifice* to the Lord.

Again, we see the attempt at spiritualizing disobedience and the shift in who was to blame. Also, we see that the sacrifice was not right. It was not accepted by the Lord. The animals were taken from wicked men and wicked territory. Saul's men wanted to sacrifice to the Lord animals that resulted from their direct disobedience.

Might I say that Cain was attempting to offer God that which was a result from his direct disobedience? Perhaps he ignored the offering instructions and perhaps he had previous sin.

Ownership

Besides excellence and type, only Abel's offering indicates **ownership** by the use of the word "his." He brought from the firstlings of *his* flock. The word *his* implies that there are other flocks of sheep that are *not his*.

In keeping with the idea that Abel and his family may have been in "business" together, it is possible that Abel may have cared for flocks other than his own. He may have had a portion of sheep that were his personal flock while other sheep belonged to family members. Perhaps he exchanged care of their sheep for food or other necessities. How ever it worked, Abel presented firstlings from *his* own flock.

Cain's offering does not indicate ownership, which causes questions as to where the fruit came from. The pride in Cain may have come from growing and laboring over these specific crops that he presented to the Lord. However, just because he grew them does not mean that they were *his* to give away.

Perhaps the fruit came from his parents' lot which he also helped work. Or maybe it came by skimming from the top of each person's daily crops that were typically collected and traded for other items? One from this pile, one or two from that pile and before Cain knew it, he had compiled a gift to the Lord for which he did not have to "sacrifice."

Sin comes with a price. It is costly. A sacrifice must be made.

In 2 Samuel 24, David (king of Israel) sinned against the Lord by numbering the people. Towards the end of the chapter, David admitted his sin and knew that he had to deal with it before the Lord. He was instructed to "erect an altar on the threshing floor of Araunah the Jebusite" (24:18 NASB).

David wanted to *buy* the threshing floor but Araunah offered David to use the threshing floor and take oxen for *free*. David declared, "No, but I will surely buy it from you for a price, for I will not offer burnt offerings to the LORD my God which cost me nothing" (v.24 NASB).

Perhaps Cain's offering cost *him* nothing. Perhaps he didn't care if the price came at *another's* expense.

Abel, on the other hand, gave up what was near and dear to him. The very same sheep that he was *called* to *care for* and *tend to* were the ones that needed to be *slaughtered and consumed.* Abel was a talented shepherd, but he did not approach God with his strength and ability of "keeping the sheep." Although Abel gave his best sheep, he did not approach God as a sheep showman. Instead Abel approached God with the unfamiliar hardship of surrendering his sheep. He approached in humility.

Though sheep may have been kept (in part) for the slaughter, this shepherding occupation was hardly established yet. Abel was seemingly the one who had to go through all the "firsts" (or maybe "seconds") in this particular field.

I don't think that bloodshed was something in which Abel had previous experience. Death itself was a new occurrence to which Abel may have had little witness. When Abel gave up his sheep for the slaughter, he did not give God what was easy or natural. What he gave may have been difficult, uncomfortable and seemingly unreasonable.

Could this have been similar to the account of Abraham and Isaac, where God told Abraham to do what seemed illogical; that is, offer his son as a burnt offering (Genesis 22:2)? Obedience is often not effortless, painless or without cost.

How the tending of sheep so relates to raising our children! We know when our babies are born that we will one day have to send them out on their own. But as their first day of college nears, their wedding day approaches or the mission field calls, knowing ahead of time does not make the day any easier. We are not experienced with that kind of letting go. Neither was Abel!

It's much easier to hold on to our strengths and display them to God (and others) in a way that we are accustomed to, than it is to surrender our weaknesses and let go of what is so precious to us in such an unfamiliar way.

What incredible things God might do if we would just give it all to Him. The temporary cost of giving God our *all* may be dear, but the reward is abundant, eternal and never regretted!

Heart of Faith

Regardless of the excellence, type and ownership of the offering, it is certain that even if Cain had brought the proper or best offering, he would not have been accepted because of his **heart**. But the passage states that *Cain* and *his offering* were not accepted and for that reason, likely both his heart and his actions were impure.

In Luke 6, we discover by the words of Jesus that a bad tree cannot bring forth good fruit. Cain's actions are a reflection of his heart; one that won't bow down.

The other assurance we have is that Abel's offering was accepted because he had a *heart of faith* (Hebrews 11:4). The questions then become, how did Abel know what was acceptable? And how was he able to live out his faith in a single, present-tense moment?

Like Cain, Abel's offering was a reflection of *his* true heart. In the same Luke passage it says that a *good* tree does not bring forth *bad* fruit, and that a tree is known *by* its fruit. Whether or not Abel was required to bring a blood sacrifice, he did because he was humble before the Lord.

Even if he had not committed some terrible act of sin, Abel was not too proud to admit that he may not *understand the error of his ways* (Psalm 19:12). He was surrendered before God with an openness to receive any corrections needed. He did not think that he had "already arrived" or become a person who was so close to God that there was no more need for improvement.

We can easily become tangled up in the idea that our

surrender has brought us to perfection or that we have no more surrendering to do. As we become closer to God, we would err at the thought that we have become *like* Him, as in, we almost *are* Him.

This is the same cord that entangled Satan when he could not balance his perfection with the humility of not being God. We forget that all of our goodness comes from Him and that our surrender to the Most High must continue.

Abel *was* close to God. Not close to *being* God, but close because God dwelt *in* him. Because of that, he was able to hear God's voice and follow His instruction. This is why the problems with Cain started long before the offerings. Cain may have physically heard God's instructions, but he spiritually dismissed them as if they had no importance.

Abel offered an acceptable sacrifice to God because of his deep *faith* in the identity of God. Hebrews 11 is what many refer to as the "faith chapter." It contains accounts of individuals from the beginning of time that acted righteously due to their incredible faith. The first person mentioned is Abel in verse four. It was by faith that he offered the sacrifice.

Verse six tells us that it is impossible to please God without *faith*. So, what does having *faith* exactly entail?

Faith is more than just feelings, more than believing in the existence of God and even expands beyond the present-tense.

Faith was more than feelings as recounted in Matthew 8. Jesus was on a boat with His disciples. He was taking a nap when a wind storm moved in. The disciples woke Jesus because of their fear. Jesus responded to them with these words, "Why are ye fearful, O ye of little faith?" (v.26).

The disciples had allowed the feeling of fear to affect them. The affect proved what kind of faith they had: little.

Strong faith is not swayed by feelings. We can't allow the chaos of what's around us to cause us to lose sight of who God really is.

> **Faith is more than feelings because it is based on a foundation that is not affected by circumstance.**

Faith is also more than believing in the existence of God because even the demons believe and tremble (James 2:19). Cain could not deny that God existed, just as the demons can't. God spoke directly to Cain. However, faith was still not found in him because faith is being certain of things unseen (Hebrews 11:1b). Cain needed to believe in the promised Seed that would redeem him.

Finally, **Faith expands beyond the present tense**. If we want to live out faith in the present, we need to establish a faith about the past and future. A faith about what has happened since the beginning and what will happen in the end gives us an unwavering faith in the midst of a present situation.

In the Bible's "faith chapter," there are several key verses that speak to a *past* and *future* faith. Verse 3 speaks of the *past* by saying, "Through faith we understand that the worlds were framed by the word of God, so that things which are seen were not made of things which do appear."

Immediately the author of Hebrews establishes that faith entails believing God as Creator. What we see with our eyes was not created by something else that we can see with our eyes. There is a mastermind behind it all that is unseen. That is why faith becomes the evidence of the unseen (v.1).

Though these Old Testament believers listed in Hebrews had not arrived to the point in history of the cross, we, in current times, look back at the cross and have that same kind of faith. There is an aspect of faith that hinges on what happened in the *past.*

Much like having faith in what already happened, there is a faith that looks to the *future.* Hebrews 11:1 states a great definition of faith by saying, "Faith is the substance of things hoped for." Hebrews 11:6b says, "he that cometh to God must believe that he is, and *that* he is a rewarder of them that diligently seek him." God is a *rewarder,* and *rewards* are dispersed *after* living out present tense faith.

Hebrews 11:13 sums up how Abel, Enoch, Noah, Abraham and Sarah were able to live out their faith. "These died in faith, not having received the promises, but having seen them *afar off,* and were persuaded of *them,* and embraced *them,* and confessed that they were strangers and pilgrims on the earth" (emphasis added). These were ordinary people who had extraordinary faith because they were persuaded of the *future.* They believed in God's promises of what was to come; that is, the promise of Jesus Christ. They had received *some* promises from God but they had not yet received the One true promise, because Jesus would come to earth generations later.

Although the cross is something that we look back on, there is a *future* faith that both these believers listed in Hebrews and we have in common: a faith about our eternal home. These individuals in Hebrews made a confession that they were strangers on earth. They did not belong to this world, but their minds were set on God's land and city above.

Look how their actions prove it. Many gave up earthly treasures which allowed them to live out a radical faith. Abel gave up his best sheep and his life for that matter. Enoch pleased God, which would have been impossible if his heart had been set on the world. Noah gave up his time, home, land and friendships. Abraham gave up any demand to know the details of where God was leading and what exactly He was doing. Sarah gave up doubts that would dismiss God as faithful. If their minds had been set on earth below, surely their actions would have revealed it. Instead, they risked it all!

As we look upward toward our true home, we dare not seek out a faith that consists of superstition, curiosity or a revelation of heavenly things that are unknown to us outside of God's Word. Rather, we seek a faith that trusts and rests in the one true God who will fulfill His promises of the final defeat of Satan and the preparation of a city where we will forever dwell with Him.

Though we are on the other side of the cross, there still remains a faith in what is to come. Looking back on these men and women of the Old Testament, we see more clearly the complete picture God was creating.

Jesus certainly fulfills that picture but the end times are yet to come. We are a part of a scene that has yet to play out. Living out a radical faith is needed *now* like it was needed *then* for those listed in Hebrews. How much more possible is it to have that faith now that we have been made complete in Christ? We certainly have no excuse!

So, how can we live out our faith in a single, present-tense moment? How can we maintain a lifestyle that acts with surrender? The book of Hebrews tells us how and gives plenty of examples, including that of Abel.

We trust in the all-encompassing identity of God. We humbly surrender to God with a confidence that rests on what He did in the *past* and trusts Him for what He will do in the *future* so that we can faithfully obey Him in the *present*!

Faith in the all-encompassing identity of God, both past and future, is how we live out complete faith in the present.

Just as we can live out *faith* in a single present-tense moment, we can act by *crisis* in a single present-tense moment. We can act with insecurity, instability or uncertainty. The key to whether we act by faith or by crisis is in the subject of time. What we *believe* concerning the times of the past and the future will dictate how we *live* in the present.

Satan is threatened by time because God has been in every bit of it and Satan hasn't. He's also threatened because God controls time and he doesn't. Beyond that, he knows his time is short. Because he is threatened, he seeks to use time as a tool to get us to live by crisis. Satan wants us to mentally live in a *past* world that already occurred or live in a *future* world that has never existed.

Although God has a beautiful *past* of Himself for you to look back on (His beginning as Alpha, His creation and His death and resurrection), Satan has a hideous *past* for you to focus on (your failures, your losses and painful memories). God wants you to recall that He has delivered you from those past moments and Satan wants you to relive them.

Though God has an abundant and eternal *future* for you to set your mind on (the earthly plans He has for you to fulfill, heaven, and life everlasting with Him), Satan has a disturbing and corruptible *future* for you to think on (worries, anxiety and stress about tomorrow or about what others will think of you).

God wants to bring comfort and relief to your mind by reminding you of His promises for the future and His faithfulness to you in times past. Satan wants to bring confusion and stress to your mind so that you live in uncertainty. Psalm 94:19 says, "When my anxious thoughts multiply within me, Your consolations delight my soul" (NASB).

Satan's goal is to *waste your present*. He wants you to live in your past failures or future worries so that you are not useful in the moments that you are in.

God's purpose is to make you *useful and fruitful in the present*. Your present moments may consist of challenges, joys, sorrows, celebrations or hurts, but He has a journey for you through which you can grow, learn, change and impact in all of these.

God has other moments He wants you to live out. Each day brings more. Keep moving forward with God. Look to His beginning and His eternity to live the most abundant present possible. Be thankful for all God has delivered you from in the past and trust that He holds the future. If you do, your present moments will be lived out in faith. Your heart will be secure and unwavering.

What we believe about who God is will directly affect who we believe we are! It will affect how we act or react in a single present-tense moment. Will we act by faith or by crisis? **My Faith: Past and Future, My Faith: Present!** Predetermine who you believe God has always been and forever will be!

Remember that without faith, our offerings cannot please God. We all desire acceptance, but a problem comes into play when we either seek acceptance from the *wrong source* (being people pleasers) or we attempt to fool the *right source* (God).

Cain attempted to *fool* the right source but Abel had *faith* in the right source—the complete identity of God. As a result, he and his offering were accepted. God regarded him. He gazed on the heart of Abel. He delighted to look it over.

Psalm 119:117 uses the same word *shaah* (regard) as God used for Abel, "Uphold me that I may be safe, that I may have regard for Your statutes continually" (NASB). I think Abel's deep regard for God led him to give an offering in faith. I think God regarded Abel, not because he was perfect, but because Abel's heart gazed on and believed in God's identity. His present act of faith was anchored by predetermined faith!

Have *faith* in God from beginning to end. Believe in God's past and future "bookends" to secure your present moment. Settle in your heart that God is Alpha, Creator, Savior, Omega and Builder of an eternal city with a room for you.

Chapter 4

The Storehouse

My Treasure, My Heart.

> And Cain was very wroth, and his countenance fell. And the Lord said unto Cain, Why art thou wroth? and why is thy countenance fallen? If thou doest well, shalt thou not be accepted? (Genesis 4:5b-7a)

> for where your treasure is, there your heart will be also. (Matthew 6:21 NASB)

> Keep thy heart with all diligence; for out of it *are* the issues of life. (Proverbs 4:23)

The Heart of Cain

Matthew 6:19 says, "Do not store up for yourselves treasures on earth, where moth and rust destroy, and where thieves break in and steal" (NASB).

Have you ever had anything stolen from you? Unfortunately, my family has experienced this quite a bit. From waking up to no vehicle in our driveway (later located and recovered by Syracuse Police), to coming home to a robbed house (discovered when my brother, a friend and I got off the school bus. We toured the house with a kitchen knife, an old rifle with no ammunition, and so-called karate skills), to my father's wallet being stolen out of our house (later located on the side of our road and conveniently missing the cash… of course, this was all on my wedding day), to a garage break-in and tools stolen (the dogs seemed to have slept through that one), to cash being taken out of my purse at work (which was totally caught on camera!), to my mother's entire purse being taken from her office and hidden within an old three story building (thankfully found after searching every unique nook and cranny), to our van stolen out of a church parking lot (also later located by Syracuse Police), to multiple cars ransacked in the middle of the night in our driveway (I'm not sure they found anything of value), to the recent disappearance of our 4-wheeler (which was also located by police with minimal damage)…

Between these and several other theft incidents, I can say that it is not fun, quite invasive, and flat out disturbing to be a victim.

However, what if my heart had been tied to all those earthly possessions? What if my whole identity was in all that could be taken away from me? The results would be ugly. My emotions would be wild and out of control!

Earthly treasures cannot provide security. They will fail at some point—either by rusting, decaying or being stolen. They have no eternal value. Our hearts are revealed by how we react when earthly tangibles prove to fail us.

When we seek worldly treasures...

- We're uncertain we will gain what we seek
- We're afraid we will lose what we gained
- No matter what happens, we end up empty

Matthew continues to say, "But store up for yourselves treasures in heaven, where neither moth nor rust destroys, and where thieves do not break in or steal" (6:20 NASB). The treasures of heaven will not fail us. They are enduring and can never disappoint. God is a faithful God whom we can rely on, and His internal benefits far succeed any external pleasures of the world.

When we seek heavenly treasures...

- We have confidence we will find what we seek
- We are sure we will keep what we find
- We are satisfied and fulfilled within

Matthew concludes, "for where your treasure is, there your heart will be also" (6:21 NASB). Our treasure and our heart are inseparable. We can't have one without the other. **My Treasure, My Heart!** The heart acts as a storehouse for our emotions, desires, will and thoughts. What we love and treasure the most is held in our heart. We have the choice to store earthly treasures or heavenly treasures.

Proverbs 4:23 tells us to "Keep thy heart with all diligence; for out of it *are* the issues of life." What is in our hearts comes out in our lives. When we fill our hearts with the corruptible treasures of the earth, corrupted emotions, desires, and thoughts flow from it. When we fill our hearts with heavenly treasures, good flows out in every way.

One area in which Cain had a problem was his emotions.

His emotions proved ugly because his heart was corrupted. His heart was corrupted because his treasure was earthly. His earthly treasures had infected his core, and negative emotions began to spring out of his heart.

Let's take a deeper look at emotions and how they relate to our passage.

Emotions

Satan wants to fill our *heart closets* with his line of clothing. Negative emotions can spring out of a heart that is already filled with earthly treasures; but negative emotions can also give Satan a foothold for more sin to take place. While not all negative emotions are directly sinful, the long-term wearing of them (refusal to surrender them) in our heart, is.

In Genesis 4:5b-6, Satan is at Cain's door, seeking to destroy him through his feelings. We first read, "And Cain was very wroth, and his countenance fell." In other words, he was angry and miserable because he didn't get the treasure he wanted. Yes. On the outside he was seeking God's acceptance. But on the inside, he had another treasure in mind—and God was just someone he needed to go through in order to secure it.

Cain's outward emotions (after the Lord's rejection of his offering) reveal what his initial intentions were before he gave his offering. He was seeking to fool God, but didn't get his way. As Cain remained silent with an upset "pout face," the Lord said, "Why art thou wroth? and why is thy countenance fallen?"

Over the years I've had the opportunity to work with many teenagers facing identity crises. I can recall many teens who reacted the same way as Cain when they were confronted with their disobedience. What I can tell you is that an angry, miserable look accompanied by silence came not only from disobedience, but from multiple rounds of disobedience.

The first time a person got in trouble, they gave excuses about their behavior. If the excuses didn't fool me, the next time they came up with a well thought-out defense. When that didn't trick me, they let out their raised and angry voice, which turned into an all-out verbal battle. After attempting one more round of every crafty and distracting argument they could come up with, they eventually stopped trying to fight. They realized I wasn't going to buy into their junk.

By the next time they got in trouble, all they had left was an angry, miserable blank stare with complete and utter silence. They knew they were caught. All of their tactics had been used and had gotten them nowhere.

They were mad because they didn't get away with their prior actions. They were miserable and sad because they were caught and had to deal with the consequences. They had a blank unrepentant stare because they were not going to allow any of my words of advice infiltrate them. They had allowed Satan to eat at them until they were hollow. Though I still attempted to reach out to them, they had put up a wall that was impenetrable.

Knowing what was coming down the road for Cain, I believe he had this *same* angry and miserable unrepentant, blank stare. Even though his face displayed his anger and sadness, I think his eyes revealed an empty hole. Cain was allowing his *emotions* to rule over him and Satan was at his door, just waiting to get in through the chaos of those feelings.

Perhaps this was not the first time Cain had allowed his feelings to get the better of him. Have you ever gotten far more angry than a present situation called for? I don't think the Lord's rejection of Cain's offering warrants the level of anger that should lead to murder. Perhaps there was *past* anger that Cain had never dealt with, and his *present* situation just pulled up all the archives! Perhaps Cain had been seeking the same earthly treasure for quite some time and the Lord's interference caused all that was in his heart to burst.

Besides a sad and angry face, my guess is that other emotions were bubbling inside Cain as well. Let's take a look at some emotions that, if not dealt with, can turn us into the "Cain-like" person we don't want to become.

Anger

When the subject of anger arises, many have clung to the verse found in Ephesians that says, "Be ye angry, and sin not: let not the sun go down upon your wrath" (Ephesians 4:26). What many take away from this verse is that it is okay to get angry. The truth is, it's only okay to get angry if you do not sin.

The danger with anger is that most of us cannot get angry without thinking evil thoughts about a person, ripping them to shreds verbally, or just acting poorly on that feeling. This is why anger needs to be dealt with right away. The end of the day brings with it an expiration that, if surpassed, will spoil the character of your heart.

The following verse in Ephesians says, "Neither give place to the devil" (v.27). The word *place* means "opportunity, power, occasion for acting."[7] In other words, don't give the devil a good occasion to show up in your life and take over. Anger does that. It gives a great occasion.

We have forgotten so many other verses that instruct us about anger, like, "He that is slow to anger is better than the mighty; and he that ruleth his spirit than he that taketh a city" (Proverbs 16:32). Or what about these verses?

"Wherefore, my beloved brethren, let every man be swift to hear, slow to speak, slow to wrath: For the wrath of man worketh not the righteousness of God" (James 1:19). "But now ye also put off these; anger, wrath, malice, blasphemy, filthy communication out of your mouth" (Colossians 3:8).

If anger is something we should put off, then it isn't something we should readily have in our heart's closet to put on. Cain chose to put on the clothes of anger that he likely (in years past) had sewn for quite some time. In fact, not only did he already have them available in his closet from previous uses, but I think he was just dying for an excuse to walk down the runway with them!

Bitterness

Bitterness is what happens when you don't deal with anger. It's when anger makes a comfortable home in your heart. Bitterness is anger that has settled into your core. The longer it sits there, the more solidified it becomes. The harder it gets, the harder it is to break up.

Ephesians 4:31 reminds us, "Let all bitterness and wrath and anger and clamor and slander be put away from you, along with all malice" (NASB). Get it out of your heart's closet! The sooner, the better.

Fear

The feeling of fear is another piece of clothing that Satan would love for us to sew. The pattern of fear is easy. It's like a thick, dark fabric that encases our entire body head to toe. It's certainly not comfortable or breathable. Rather, it's tight and gripping.

Psalm 34:4 says, "I sought the LORD, and he heard me, and delivered me from all my fears." Psalm 56:3-4 says, "When I am afraid, I will put my trust in You. In God, whose word I praise, In God I have put my trust; I shall not be afraid. What can mere men do to me?" (NASB). When we place God's *power* next to our fears, it causes us to name the fear "mere." God's *strength* makes the thing we fear look like a weakling!

Anxiety

The clothes of worry and anxiety are extremely heavy. It weighs on not only the heart, but the mind. It's like an oversized helmet on your head that your neck can't support. It restrains you from looking up and enjoying the life that is happening right in front of you. Instead, you become consumed with troubling thoughts.

Proverbs 12:25 says, "Anxiety in a man's heart weighs it down, but a good word makes it glad" (NASB). Words are powerful. They can comfort. They can help lift the helmet off. They can set our shoulders back and straighten out our posture so that we can experience and embrace the reality of the present.

Sadness

Sadness and depression have the same effect as anxiety—weight on our head. This weight is often shown in our facial expressions. Remember what the Lord said to Cain? "and why is thy countenance fallen?" (Genesis 4:6b). Cain's face displayed sadness. It was downcast.

The same word *countenance* appears in Psalm 43:5 and says, "Why are you in despair, O my soul? And why are you disturbed within me? Hope in God, for I shall again praise Him, the help of my countenance and my God" (NASB). The word *help* in this verse is the Hebrew word *Yeshuah* which means *Salvation*![8] God saves us from living in the clothes of despair. He saves us from the negative expression on our face because he saves the core of the problem: our heart.

Psalm 3:3 also says, "But thou, O LORD, *art* a shield for me; my glory, and the lifter up of mine head." God puts His hands under our chin and lifts our head up. He touches our heart and changes our countenance. He even gives our heart and mouth a new and cheerful tune to sing (Psalm 40:1-3).

Jealousy

The world (or Christians caught up in worldly ways) can often become jealous of the heart-clothes a secure Christian wears. They become jealous of your peace during troubling times and your joy during sorrowful times. They even become jealous of the evidences of God when He answers your prayers or supplies your needs.

Even though these people could receive from God in the same way, they choose not to. Instead, they carry on with their own ways yet somehow become disappointed with the results. When *a surrendered believer* receives the blessings of God that the *prideful person* desired, the prideful person becomes jealous of what they think they deserved.

It is often true that a prideful person may have more worldly benefits such as money, power or position, yet may remain jealous of the surrendered believer whose only riches, power and position exist in Christ.

Sometimes Christians become jealous of the world. Psalm 37:1,2 says "Do not fret because of evildoers, be not envious toward wrongdoers. For they will wither quickly like the grass and fade like the green herb" (NASB). Though it may seem like the clothing of the world is more fun, stylish or entertaining, it is not lasting.

Envy and Strife. Confusion and Shame.

Certainly Cain became angry when his offering was not accepted, but he allowed that to sink deeper as he churned it into a hot, steaming pot of soup called *strife* and *envy*.

Proverbs 30:33 says, "For the churning of milk produces butter, and pressing the nose brings forth blood; so the churning of anger produces strife" (NASB). Cain's *anger* had produced *conflict, dissension* and a *resentful* desire to have what his brother had.

James 3:16 tells us what clothing matches perfectly with envy and strife: "Where envying and strife is, there is confusion and every evil work."

When sin is in the mix, simple things look foggy. After the Lord addressed Cain's feelings, He said, "If thou doest well, shalt thou not be accepted?" (v.7). God was not out to make the offerings complicated. In fact, it could not have been any simpler. If Cain had done right, he would have been accepted. The complication of it only comes into play when *we choose* to complicate it. When we choose envy and strife, we choose confusion.

1 Corinthians 14:33 tells us that "God is not the author of confusion, but of peace." There is a strong connection in Scripture between confusion and shame. Jeremiah says, "We lie down in our shame, and our confusion covereth us: for we have sinned against the Lord our God, we and our fathers, from our youth even into this day, and have not obeyed the voice of the Lord our God" (Jeremiah 3:25). Later in the book, Jeremiah says that his persecutors will stumble, be ashamed, and have everlasting confusion (20:11). In Psalms we find verses like, "Let them be ashamed and brought to confusion together that rejoice at mine hurt" (35:26) and "Let mine adversaries be clothed with shame,

and let them cover themselves with their own confusion, as with a mantle" (109:29).

These verses clarify the connection between confusion and shame. Both are something with which the disobedient *clothe* themselves. *Sin* brings confusion and *sin* brings shame. Confusion and shame are both caused by *sin*. This affirms that God is *not* the author of confusion. Rather, He wrote a well-organized book of love!

Have you ever worn the outfit of envy, strife, confusion, sin and shame? Perhaps that is an outfit of the past. If Satan pulls out an old photo of you wearing these, I hope you can say, "That is so out-dated!"

Satan wants to get into our hearts through the chaos of our feelings. When our emotions begin to overtake us, we need to direct them out through our prayer time with the Lord. We need to talk about them, surrender them and at many times physically cry them out.

> **If our overwhelming emotions aren't poured up and surrendered vertically, we will end up vomiting them out horizontally.**

Humankind will suffer the consequences of our lack of surrender!

We will suffer too. Remember, God asked Cain about his negative emotions. He then told Cain that if he had done right, he would have been accepted. The word *accepted* means that Cain would have been *lifted up*. God was showing Cain that there was a connection between his negative emotions and his choice to *not* do what was right—his choice to not surrender. God *lifts up* those who humble themselves

(James 4:10). If Cain had done right through surrender, his countenance would have been *lifted up.* His face would have displayed a different look if his heart had been filled with the right treasure. **My Treasure, My Heart.**

Your heart will fill up with emotions that reflect your treasure. Earthly treasures fail us but heavenly treasures fulfill us. Earthly treasures let us down, but heavenly treasures *lift us up.*

We are often more responsible for our negative emotions that we want to acknowledge. We'd rather blame our circumstances. We'd rather declare *who else* or *what else* is responsible for the misery we feel. The truth is: we are as joyful as we are surrendered. We choose joy or misery when we choose our treasure.

This doesn't mean that life's circumstances are never sad or that we should never cry, but that we choose God to be the lifter of our head, the cure for our countenance and the healer for our hearts—before our emotions have time to take over. If we are truly seeking eternal matters, then earthly circumstances will have no grip on us.

Let's take a look at an example of a woman whose *countenance* changed after surrendering her *sadness.*

A Request and a Promise

The book of first Samuel begins with the story of a woman named Hannah. Hannah was married to a man named Elkanah who also had another wife named Peninnah. Peninnah had children but Hannah did not because the Lord had prevented her from conceiving. Peninnah taunted Hannah to stir up trouble and cause her to fret. Elkanah attempted to fulfill Hannah's needs with a double portion and his love. Instead of sympathizing with his wife's hurts, he asked her why she was so sad. He then said, "Am I not better to you than ten sons?" (1:8 NASB).

Though Hannah's response is not recorded, I can only assume the answer was, "This is not about how good you are to me."

Year after year, the family went to Shiloh to sacrifice to and worship the Lord. And year after year, Peninnah taunted Hannah as if to mock her for still going up to the house of the Lord even though He had not given her a child. Clearly, Satan was at work by bringing questions and doubts through Peninnah.

One particular year Peninnah ridiculed Hannah again. Hannah cried and refused to eat even though she was given the double portion. After dinner, Hannah went to the temple and cried her heart out to the Lord with a request and a promise. The request was for a male child and the promise was that she would give him back to the Lord for all the days of his life.

At this time, Eli, the priest, had been sitting close by in the temple and though he could not hear Hannah's words, he was watching her mouth. It appeared to Eli that Hannah was drunk and so he accused and questioned her. Hannah responded that she had not drunk any wine but had poured out her heart to the Lord.

Oh, the grief and heartache Hannah must have felt. Her heart was bursting with emotions but she decided to do the right thing with those emotions. She released them into a prayer to the Lord.

Thankfully, Eli ended up believing Hannah and stated that her request would be granted. The end of verse 18 says, "her countenance was no more sad."

I wonder if Cain had done the same thing with his anger and sadness, if his story would have also ended with his countenance being "no more sad" and "no more angry."

Even though the emotions Hannah faced began to eat at her, she decided to take them to the Lord in surrender. She asked the Lord for life and in return she would devote that life back to the Lord.

The same can happen when we face tough life situations that cause our emotions to rise. We can offer complete surrender and God will complete us like no one else can.

Through tears and brokenness, Hannah's heart bowed down that day. I think she chose the Lord as her treasure above all else.

The next day, Elkanah, Hannah, and seemingly others, rose early in the morning to worship the Lord. This is a perfect picture that there is an order to be followed. First: the surrender of our hearts. Second: the praise of our hearts. Our worship and our offering will not be right nor will it be accepted when our belief and surrender is missing or lacking. Our lips offer what our hearts are full of! (Luke 6:45). And our hearts are full of whatever treasure we seek. Hannah's heart knew that. Cain's did not.

Continuing the story, Elkanah and Hannah returned home and conceived a child. After the birth of Samuel, it was once again time for the yearly sacrifice. After they slaughtered the bullock, Hannah said, "For this child I prayed; and the Lord hath given me my petition which I asked of him: Therefore also I have lent him to the LORD; as long as he liveth he shall be lent to the LORD" (1:27-28). In chapter 2 she continued to pray, saying, "My heart rejoiceth in the Lord" (2:1).

I can clearly recall multiple rounds of surrender with a petition for God to give my husband and I a child. Part of our journey was God leading us in a practical way that would eventually allow the possibility of having a child, and the other part was surrendering to the sovereignty of

God, knowing it was He who controlled all things and not a physician.

Though a doctor can give you percentages and statistics about a possible outcome, it was God who told me something different. He said, "The lot is cast into the lap; but the whole disposing thereof *is* of the LORD" (Psalm 16:33). In other words, God has total control of the outcome!

I can remember my final surrender. It was final because even though I had surrendered pieces of the journey to God along the way, I was finally surrendering *completely.* I was letting God have full control and trusting that His way was the best way. Though I had other previous days of tears, I was finally releasing all of my emotions and heartaches up to God.

I still came to the Lord with a request for a child and a promise to give that child back to Him for all of its days, but that promise would not have been valid if I had not surrendered *completely.* I could not offer a child to the Lord if I was not offered up to Him *first.*

We know that God does not always answer in the way that we want Him to. The surrender is a surrender to whatever He decides. Our treasure must be in Him and Him alone. In the case of Hannah and myself, He granted our request and therefore, we will uphold our promise.

As for Hannah's son, he became the last judge. He was the last because the people of Israel demanded a king to lead them. Samuel anointed both the first and second king of Israel: Saul and David.

As for my son, I have lent him back to the Lord. I am continually grateful and surrendered. My heart rejoices!

If you feel negative or uncontrollable emotions bubbling

up inside of you, you need to check your treasures. You need to check your heart. Before those emotions get loose to do whatever they freely choose, decide to surrender them up to God. Give God control over your heart. Let Him have His way in you!

The Heart of Abel

Abel had done right with his offering and therefore he was accepted. Because he was accepted, his countenance was lifted up. Abel was already experiencing the benefits of living surrendered to God. Both the character and emotions flowing from his heart were good because his treasure was good.

Here's a look inside his heart…

Fruit:

It all starts with the heart apparel of fruit. As you mature in Christ, these fruits begin to flourish within the garden of you!

In Galatians 5:22,23 we learn the list of the fruit of the Spirit which is love, joy, peace, longsuffering, gentleness, goodness, faith, meekness and temperance.

Let's take a closer look at what these fruits are all about:

Joy

The apparel of joy is permanent. It's not something we rip off when tough circumstances come our way. This piece of apparel is deep within our souls. We have joy in who God is and we have joy because we know who we are in Him. Joy is displayed on our face in the utmost sincere way.

Peace

This heart apparel brings a true rest for the soul. It takes the place of strife, envy and contention. When we surrender to God, our once disturbed spirits take on a soothing calm. There is relief, harmony and contentment. Wearing this piece changes how we relate to others.

Long-suffering

This apparel is quite durable. It is so deeply rooted in the heart that life's weary conditions do not affect its quality. It also remains steady and patient when dealing with people who would have otherwise been a cause of weariness. Those who wear this piece are often described as easygoing, flexible and uncomplaining.

Gentleness

This word means kindness. It's a virtue that has consideration for others. Beyond consideration, wearing kindness attracts those who have been beaten down by kindness' enemy: selfishness. Kindness brings about opportunities to demonstrate God's love to those who desperately need it.

Goodness

Goodness is a trait that seeks to accomplish the goal of producing "good" in everything said or done. It goes against what would bring harm or hurt to others. There is purity, honesty, integrity and morality in the person who wears goodness.

Faith

Wearing faith not only means having faith in God but being a faithful individual. As we trust in God, we can become a person who is trustworthy. Both our words and our actions can be relied on by others.

Meekness

This word means having humility and demonstrating submission to God. Pride is wiped out by meekness, which gives us the ability to listen to the voice of God, receive His correction and meet the needs of those around us. Wearing meekness is essential. This piece will help us put on more pieces of Godly clothing.

Temperance

This apparel means having self control over worldly passions and desires. It's not "self" that you put on to have control. It's by putting on temperance that makes self-control possible. When we wear these clothes, we can walk steadily, maintain our equilibrium and keep our composure. People who wear temperance are self-disciplined, have clarity of mind and use discretion before acting or reacting.

Love

The fruit of love is a summary of all the other fruits that we can put on. 2 John 1:6 reminds us that love is walking after God's commandments. The greatest two commandments contain the word *love*—love God, love others.

1 John 4:19 says, "We love him, because he first loved us." Here's how the chain of love works. Because God loved us, we can love Him; by loving Him, we can love others! 1 John chapter three says, "that we should love one another. Not as Cain ..." (vv.11b-12). Cain was an example of all that is opposite of love. The proof that he did not love God was in the fact that he did not love man.

Want to check your love levels for God? Start by checking your love levels for others. It simply will not lie.

As we consider the Fruits of the Spirit, we can easily look in the mirror and, if honest, can identify if we are wearing these fruits. They are not each a different outfit but rather, they make up a whole outfit. If *temperance* were a set of pants, we wouldn't dare leave home without them!

What fruits do you resist wearing? Make a full connection to the Holy Spirit to grow these fruits in your life. These fruits are the benefits that we harvest from living surrendered!

Armor

When we come to know Christ as Savior, the Halloween costumes (false identities) in our heart's closet empty out and the Fruit of the Spirit begins to take its place. In addition to fruit, we need to guard our hearts with some pretty tough protective gear.

Ephesians 6 lists the essential pieces of this gear; the belt of truth, the breastplate of righteousness, the shoes of the gospel of peace, the shield of faith, the helmet of salvation and the sword of the Spirit.

Sometimes we forget how important this armor is. We walk around acting like the devil doesn't exist or that he isn't active. Satan *does* exist and he has come down to earth with a great wrath because even he knows that his days are numbered (Revelation 12:12).

In the meantime, we are fighting a battle. And who would walk around a battle field with missing armor? There are six essential pieces that will help you win. All of these pieces are crucial. In fact, just before they are listed, we are told to put them on *completely*. The whole armor is needed so that we can "stand against the schemes of the devil" (Ephesians 6:11 NASB).

Belt of Truth

A belt is something you wrap around yourself. It holds other pieces of clothing in place and makes taking action focused because you don't have to worry about those pieces loosening, falling down or restricting your movements. This belt makes you prepared to take action. Studying God's word and truth will make you ready for the spiritual battle you'll face.

Breastplate of Righteousness

This is a plate over the front of you that protects all the major organs of the body. The expectation is that you won't turn your back to the enemy and retreat. Instead, you stand firm and fight because the righteousness that we have is not ours but Christ's (Philippians 3:9) and He cannot be defeated.

Shoes of the Gospel of Peace

Shoes are needed for protection against rocks, traps or other obstacles that could cut, scrape or injure our feet. The shoes also represent the foundation on which our faith stands; the gospel. The idea about peace is that although we march into battle fighting the chaos of the enemy, God gives our mind peace because we are founded on the gospel message that has solidified an end of victory for us.

Shield of Faith

This was a large shield (4 x 2.5 feet) that you would be able to crouch behind for protection from enemy arrows. This shield was solid and likely made out of wood. A soldier would have to cling tight to it without loosening his grip. In the same way, our faith needs to be solid with a tight grip and reliance on Jesus so that Satan's arrows will be blocked.

Helmet of Salvation

This helmet blocks all false doctrine and lies that are aimed at our minds. What filters through our minds will come out of our mouth. This is why it is important to keep our helmets on in a snug fit position.

Sword of the Spirit

This piece of armor is offensive. Jesus defeated Satan in the wilderness with this sword as it is the Word of God. If we don't use our swords, they become rusty and dull. Instead we recall that iron sharpens iron (Proverbs 27:17). We need to study and know the Bible. We need to surround ourselves with others whom we can grow sharper. This sword is the Word of God alive in us through His Holy Spirit.

Remember that in this battle, we are not alone. God is with us and even fights for us. Many go into physical battle and cannot predict the outcome, but we go into spiritual battle knowing that we are on the winning side. There is no reason for fear. Satan will be overcome.

We can examine the storehouse of our heart by observing the thoughts which rule our minds, the emotions displayed on our face and the character shown in our actions. When we are honest about what is flowing out of us, we can get honest about the core of the problem within us.

God addressed the outward problem of Cain's negative

emotions to show him there was a deeper problem in his storehouse!

As we examine the storehouse of our own heart, we need to question whether or not it has become a blend of good fruit and rotten garbage. For some of us, our armor is tucked away in the back and we have become injured in the battle.

What I want to know is—when will October be over for us? When will Halloween end? When will we give up the costumes of false identities in our closet? When will we move on to spring? When will we let Good Friday and Resurrection Day play on "repeat" in our heart? When will we give up the heart-clothes of Cain and put on the heart-apparel of Abel? When will we fill our hearts with fruit and armor? When will we surrender our emotions and let God be the lifter of our head?

Today is a good day to begin storing something new!

Chapter 5

Breathe

Change My Treasure, Change My Heart

> and if thou doest not well, sin lieth at the door. And unto thee shall be his desire, and thou shalt rule over him. (Genesis 4:7b)

> LOVE THE LORD YOUR GOD WITH ALL YOUR HEART. (Luke 10:27a NASB)

> The Spirit of God has made me, And the breath of the Almighty gives me life. (Job 33:4 NASB)

Change Your Treasure, Change Your Heart

After the Lord explained that if Cain had done what was right, he would have been accepted, He said, "And if thou doest not well, sin lieth at the door. And unto thee shall be his desire, and thou shalt rule over him" (Genesis 4:7). Cain did not do what was right. The sin that "lieth" at Cain's door literally means that it was hunched over, like an animal on all fours, ready to pounce at its prey. Sin was licking its chops with desire for a tasty meal.

Cain had gotten to the point where his refusal to surrender to the Lord would equal Satan ruling over him. Look how the passage changes from describing sin as a *"what"* to sin as a *"who." Sin* was at the door but Cain needed to rule over *him*. There was something deeper behind the surface sin. There was an unseen force at work in Cain. The force was the cause of the sin and *he* needed to be ruled over.

God was telling Cain that there was a *master* behind the sin working in him and logically, he would need *another master* working in him in order to conquer it. In other words…

The way to rule over Satan is by allowing God to rule over you!

I think Cain was the kind of guy who said "I can" to everything. I think Cain thought he was so talented that he believed there was nothing he couldn't take on. When God told Cain to rule over Satan, He was directing Cain to do what was completely impossible to do without Him. God was telling Cain to rule over Satan so that Cain might come to the realization that there was something he couldn't do on his own—something he had already failed at and needed help to accomplish.

God gave Cain the opportunity to conclude, "I can't. I need You, Lord!" God was prompting Cain to admit he had a weakness. Cain needed to admit that he had no power over the enemy unless he surrendered to the only One who did!

If Cain refused to allow God to rule over him, more sin would be in his future. Because Cain had never placed his trust in God, he needed to take the first step of Salvation. "Ye are of God, little children, and have overcome them: because greater is he that is in you, than he that is in the world" (1 John 4:4).

He has to be *in you* first. This is the start of uncovering your true identity. This is how Cain's heart could change from submitting to the negative emotions that had been ruling it, to the fruits of the Spirit that reigned in Abel. This is how Cain's countenance could be lifted up. This is how Cain could change his treasure. **Change My Treasure, Change My Heart.**

Saying "My Treasure" is like saying "My God." Our treasure is what we love the most! The statement is really, **My God, My Heart.** Change who my god is, change how my heart is. Cain needed to give up the god of himself who had no ability to rule over Satan and surrender to the God of the Universe who already conquered the enemy!

If you won't admit you have a weakness, you won't admit you need a Savior!

Completely

Among The Thirsty is a contemporary Christian band that seeks to reach others with the Gospel of Christ through their music. Front-man Ryan Daniel and I grew up attending the same summer Bible camp in Oswego, NY as kids.

Upon visiting the camp grounds this past summer, Ryan played and sang one of the band's newest songs at the closing program called "Completely." If you haven't heard it yet, I'd encourage you to check it out.

This song touched me on a personal level as I have had to cry out similar words to the Lord several times in my.life.

After playing it a few times, something struck me. I couldn't help but think that these were the words that Cain *could* have spoken between verses seven and eight in Genesis 4.

After the Lord addressed Cain's emotions, warned him of enemy presence and instructed him on how to defeat Satan, Cain stood in the most defining moment of his life. He was floating in the middle of two verses and possible outcomes.

Verse seven is what we just covered. In verse eight, Cain talked with his brother. What happened in the moments in between these two verses is crucial to how the next major scene is permanently recorded in Scripture. We are at a pivotal climax in Cain's story! The tension is high. The emotion is overflowing. The results will prove extreme.

When I hear the song "Completely," I think how this is the heart cry that Cain could have released to the Lord instead of directing his anger toward his brother. Put yourself in Cain's shoes and just imagine that he responded to the Lord's correction and advice with these words. Read the lyrics or even listen to the song and imagine that before talking with Abel, Cain approached God with this broken heart cry:

[1]I'm feeling so small
Standing here weeping
As I'm coming clean
Of the secrets I'm keeping

I've caused so much pain
To the ones I love the most
And I'm falling apart
As I carry my heart to Your throne

I am completely surrendering
Finally giving You everything
You're my redeemer, I run to the cross
Because You are more than enough
Lord complete me
Cause I'm Yours completely

I'm letting go
There's nothing I own
The treasures I held
Just weighed down my soul
And there's nothing left
Inside of me
But a longing for You
And a longing to be the man that You need

I am completely surrendering
Finally giving You everything
You're my redeemer, I run to the cross
Because You are more than enough
Lord complete me
Cause I'm Yours completely

I let Your gifts take the place of you
But You pulled up my selfishness from it's roots
Now I am a broken and fragile me
But I'm where You want me to be

I am completely surrendering

Finally giving You everything
You're my redeemer, I run to the cross
Because You are more than enough
Lord complete me
Cause I'm Yours completely
Lord complete me
Cause I'm Yours completely[9]

Oh, how I wish Cain had spoken these words. How I wish he could have let go of his pride and made this his hearts lament! His upcoming conversation with Abel would have looked much different.

Some of you, like me, are reading the lyrics of this song and thinking of a time when God somehow got a hold of your heart and you surrendered. You are astounded at how close you were to remaining as a "Cain" or how close you were to holding onto all your "Cain-like" qualities.

Instead, words like these flowed from your heart, out of your lips and up to the ears of Jesus. Some of you are not even sure how He reached you. Some of you were headed straight for utter darkness and then His sovereign light opened your eyes.

My heart breaks for the "Cain's" of this world who find themselves at this defining moment that our Cain from Genesis was facing. They've been rebellious and even wicked but God is still giving them an opportunity to turn their life around. The next move is crucial and as much as we can pour *our* heart out before the Lord, we cannot pour *their* heart out for them. They must make their own choice and therefore reap the consequence or reward.

Cain is at a stand-still moment, but he must make a move. He could confess his sin, admit his wrong and ask for forgiveness. He could pour out a heart cry with the release of his anger and other emotions. He could let go of the temporary things of this world and cling onto God for all eternity. He could lay down the weights and secrets that have imprisoned him. He could let God clean out his closet of false identities. He could surrender himself along with the gifts and talents God had given him. He could let God pull up the weeds that entangled him.

> **The man who was so skilled at tilling the ground, needed to let God be the tiller of his heart!**

Cain could say, "Forget the fruit offering. First, I give you my heart." He could say, "Forget my burdensome earthly treasures. I desire the uplifting treasure of You!" He could say, "I'm broken. I'm hollow. I'm weak. I need You." He could say, "I'm done wanting You to just 'top me off' so that I can look good to others. I empty myself before You so that You can truly fill me up." He could say, "God, I want You and I long to have the identity You have for me."

He could say, "Lord, I surrender. I need You to be complete!"

You will never live like you're complete without surrendering. You were made for God. You were made to bring Him glory. You were made to live out surrender.

If you don't, then you will continually wander in search for completeness yet never find it. You will have free-will, all right, but to choose against surrendering generates an emptiness that no one and nothing can fill.

It's time to be made whole. It's time to be made complete. It's time to breathe!

Breathe

Becoming complete resembles the breathing process. As we physically breathe, we must spiritually breathe, too. We must *breathe in God* and we must *breathe out self.*

Physically speaking, breathing is essential to life. Not only do our bodies need oxygen, but our blood needs to remove waste. This is all accomplished by proper breathing. Without it, we cannot thrive.

When we physically breathe in, we take air into our lungs. Our diaphragm contracts downward to create space for our lungs to expand. Oxygen passes through different parts of the body to make its way to the heart and the heart takes it through our bloodstream to the rest of our body. Spiritually speaking, we need to fill up on God in the core of our hearts so that He can move through us and impact every part of our body.

When we physically breathe out, our diaphragm relaxes and moves upward. It puts pressure on our lungs and drives the air out of us. Spiritually speaking, we need to surrender our self. We need to breathe out and release to God all that we tightly want to hold back. This surrender process relaxes us. It gives us peace.

Breathing in God produces our *identity* and breathing out self produces our *surrender* to Him. Before Salvation, we are essentially walking around as dead people—not spiritually breathing. Before being made alive by God's grace, we are dead in our sins (Ephesians 2:5).

Just as we take our first breath as we enter this world as a baby, we must take our first breath as we enter into an eternal relationship with Jesus. Once we take our first spiritual breath, we are forever alive. Just as a baby continues to breathe after the first breath, we spiritually keep breathing as well. The first breath gives us confirmation of everlasting life but the following breaths help us grow and mature in our walk. As the years of breathing go by, we go from baby to toddler to kid to young adult to mature adult.

Spiritual breathing is an endless cycle that we continue in order to live and live completely. We must keep believing *God* and we must keep surrendering *self*. Our spiritual quality of life on earth is determined by how well we are spiritually breathing.

Let's talk about a few factors of continued breathing…

Holding our Breath

If we were to take a deep breath of God *in* and not let self *out*, we'd be holding our breath while a battle rages within us. Meanwhile, we turn red in the face from lack of oxygen. We are about to blow at any minute. Self must come out!

Once self does come out, it comes out with a major release, followed by several gasps of air until our breathing becomes steady again. It's good that "self" came out, but there are still repercussions to having held our breath in the first place.

If we were to let out all of self but not breathe God in again, we'd still be holding our breath but this time, we become weak. Like exhausting much air into an inner tube for the pool, we become lightheaded with an emptiness that overwhelms us.

In our spiritual life, we can often get caught up in exhausting all of our efforts into ministry without spending our own personal time with God. We need refueling. We must breathe God in again!

Holding our breath spiritually is like holding our breath physically. We often (without hardly realizing) attempt to stretch our muscles while holding our breath. However, when we do this, not enough oxygen is being carried to our muscles. The purpose of our stretching is almost pointless and the risk of injury is at stake!

Whatever we do, we must do it while breathing. We need to believe God and let go of the fleshly waste within us. When we do, we can live for God in the best possible way. With His strength, we can fulfill His purpose and plan for our lives!

Short and Quick

Sometimes we attempt to take short, quick breaths in and out. This becomes tiresome real fast. Try it. We want a little bit of God and then we are willing to let a little bit of self out. There is nothing more unfulfilling. In fact, I think I feel a headache coming on!

The Wheeze

Wheezing while breathing in and out is the equivalent of spiritual asthma and hinders our spiritual health. Reaching for an inhaler for a quick fix will not heal the ailment long term. We need a complete dose of the Healer to be able to breathe right again. We need a dose of the One who can create permanent changes in us.

The Obstruction

If breathing becomes difficult, it may be because there is an obstruction to the airways. This happened to God's people in the book of Esther. God's people were threatened with their last days of breathing because a wicked man was willing to pay money for the destruction of the Jews. Esther (the Queen) was a Jew herself and had been strategically placed by God in a position that could help save the life of God's people. However, Esther would be taking a major risk by approaching the king on this matter.

Mordecai (Esther's uncle who had raised her) told Esther that God would provide *enlargement* and deliverance to the Jews by another means if Esther refused to speak to the king about the scheduled death of the Jews (Esther 4:14). He also challenged Esther to fulfill her destiny despite her fears. He practically said, "Baby, you were born for this moment!"

Either way, God was going to give His people *enlargement*. The word *enlargement* means, *respite,*[10] as in *respiration*. God was going to provide room for the Jews to continue to breathe despite the obstacle they faced. It was as if God's people had something lodged in their throat hindering them from breathing well, and God was going to *enlarge* that space. He was going to open up the airways. Physically speaking, it was as if He was going to enlarge the trachea, move the diaphragm downward and place a vacuum in the lungs that would suck the air in.

Obstacles occur in all of our lives. They seek to stop us from breathing in God and breathing out self. But God is bigger than any obstacle. If an obstruction fills our entire throat, God can enlarge the space. He is a *big God* who can do *big things*. He is not confined to man's spatial understanding.

Psalms 18:36 reminds us, "You enlarge my steps under me, And my feet have not slipped" (NASB).

Complete Breathing

What we should do is take long, deep breaths of God *in* and release all of self *out*. Breathing in God comes in many forms. It may be reading and soaking in His Word, listening to godly music, hearing encouraging words from a friend, listening to a message at church, sitting silent before the Lord, beholding His creation or some unexpected God-intervening moment.

Breathing out self is simply a moment of surrender within

the heart. It can happen anywhere and it can outwardly look different for each individual. It may happen in a private moment at home before the Lord or it may show up through honest, raw words in a supportive group. Some may cry and others may not. Some may fall flat on their face before God and some may stand with their hands raised toward heaven. No matter how you portray surrender outwardly, a heart bowed down looks the same inwardly.

Spiritual breathing is essential. Breathing in God produces our *identity* because we were made in His image. When we know Him, we can begin to know ourselves. Breathing out self produces our *surrender* because we are giving ourselves over to Him. After we know who He is and who we are, we are then yielding to it. We need God *completely*. As He increases, we decrease (John 3:30).

Like physical breathing, we cannot attempt to hold our breath spiritually without doing damage. Complete breaths in and out with consistency produces faithfulness and a life that is well pleasing to God. This kind of breathing is an everyday, every-moment essential for spiritual life. To invite God to fill you up and complete you is to breath *in*. To completely surrender to God is to breath *out*. Keep breathing it over and over.

As for Cain, his problem was that he simply wasn't breathing. Cain was spiritually dead. In the context of our upcoming Genesis verse where Cain will talk with Abel (v.8), dead people don't talk very well. Dead people have no substance. Cain needed to make the choice to breathe in God and breathe out self. Only then would his conversation with his brother be a healthy one.

Abel had already made the choice to breathe. He had previously believed God and surrendered to Him. I believe he had been in that breathing process for quite some time. We may be all too quick to forget that if Abel had not been spiritually breathing, he would have been as wicked as Cain! Just as the story would have turned out differently had Cain chosen to spiritually breathe, the story would have turned out differently had Abel chosen to remain spiritually dead.

From Death to Breath

Let's look at an example of two brothers who made every attempt to spiritually breathe on their own accord yet remained dead until they surrendered.

Charles Wesley, who was number eighteen out of nineteen children, grew up in England in the 1700's. He was born prematurely and his parents thought it likely that he would die (as several of their other babies previously had), but Charles continued to breathe.

As Charles grew up, he became close to his older brother, John. Both Charles and John attended Christ Church College. Charles helped form a "Holy Club" there and John would later join it. Both men grew in their religious beliefs, became ordained as preachers, wrote countless poems and hymns and even ventured out on a missions trip to the United States.

Upon returning to London from Georgia, John wrote this:

> I went to America to convert the Indians, but, O! who shall convert me who, what is he that will deliver me from this evil 'heart of unbelief I have a fair summer religion; I can talk well, nay, and believe myself, while no danger is near; but let death look me in the face, and my spirit is troubled. Nor can I say, to die is gain… I show my faith by my

> works, by staking my all upon it. I would do so again and again a thousand times, if the choice were still to make. Whoever sees me sees I would be a Christian … But in a storm I think, What if the Gospel be not true … O who will deliver me from this fear of death … Where shall I fly from it?[11]

The brothers had known for some time that something was missing despite their religious acts. They feared death because they were not spiritually alive and breathing. Their journals reveal their ongoing struggle to find faith.

Thankfully, their search came to a head in 1738. On May 21, Charles took his first spiritual breath while sick in bed. One of the scriptures he read just prior to his conversion was Psalm 40:3, "and he hath put a new song in my mouth, *even* praise unto our God: many shall see *it*, and fear, and shall trust in the LORD."

The day after his conversion, he wrote this:

> Under his protection I waked next morning, and rejoiced in reading the 107th Psalm, so nobly describing what God had done for my soul. I fell asleep again, and waked out of a dream that I was fighting two devils; had one under my feet; the other faced me some time, but faded, and sunk, and vanished away, upon my telling him I belonged to Christ.[12]

The day after that, he wrote this:

> I waked under the protection of Christ, and gave myself up, soul and body, to him. At nine I began an hymn upon my conversion,

> but was persuaded to break oil, for fear of pride. Mr. Bray coming, encouraged me to proceed in spite of Satan. I prayed Christ to stand by me, and finished the hymn. Upon my afterwards showing it to Mr. Bray, the devil threw in a fiery dart, suggesting, that it was wrong, and I had displeased God. My heart sunk within me; when, casting my eye upon a Prayer-book, I met with an answer for him. "Why boastest thou thyself, thou tyrant, that thou canst do mischief" Upon this, I clearly discerned it was a device of the enemy to keep back glory from God.[13]

The next day the Spirit was on John and at ten at night, he said, "I believe."[14] He wrote in his journal, "I felt my heart strangely warmed. I felt I did trust in Christ, Christ alone for salvation."[15]

Two brothers who had done much good were finally able to rejoice in a work much greater than anything they could ever do on their own—the work of Jesus Christ. Grace, mercy, peace and faith had anchored them as they believed on God alone for Salvation.

The hymn that Charles wrote the same year of his conversion, "And Can It Be," is my absolute favorite. The first line asks, "And can it be that I should gain an interest in the Savior's blood?" with a well-known ending line of "Amazing love! How can it be, that Thou, my God, shouldst die for me?"[16] Continuing on, it is verse three that hits home for me.

He left His Father's throne above
So free, so infinite His grace-
Emptied Himself of all but love,

And bled for Adam's helpless race:
'Tis mercy all, immense and free,
For O my God, it found out me!
'Tis mercy all, immense and free,
For O my God, it found out me![17]

This hymn reveals the depth of the change in Charles that year. It was grace that was previously missing. It was the blood of Jesus, a gift so free, that he lacked. There was nothing Charles could ever do to earn his Salvation but rather it was the mercy of God that found him out. His previous works were like an attempt to stretch his muscles without breathing.

The last verse of Charles' hymn states, "No condemnation now I dread; Jesus, and all in Him, is mine; Alive in Him, my living Head, And clothed in righteousness divine."[18] Charles' own righteousness had gotten him nowhere. He finally decided to take the offer of being clothed in the righteousness of Christ. His religion and works had not saved him; Jesus had. From that moment on, Charles was alive! He had taken his first spiritual breath.

Believing God should never cease. Surrendering to Him is an ongoing process. The more we believe God and the more we surrender self, the more of a complete life we live on earth.

Breathing goes all the way back to the beginning of time. On the sixth day of creation, when Abel's father was formed, God "breathed into his nostrils the breath of life" (Genesis 2:7). God breathed Himself into us first! It's now time to breathe out surrender to our Creator.

And then… do it all over again… and again, and again!

> **As often as you physically breathe in, spiritually believe God. As often as you physically breathe out, spiritually surrender to Him.**

If Cain was spiritually dead, then it's because he was serving a dead god. There is only one God who has life power. There is only one God who can make us spiritually breathe. There is only one God who can fill our lungs and get our hearts pumping! Cain needed to change which god ruled his heart.

Which part of God's identity are you *not* breathing in? What part of self are you unwilling to let out? Ever wonder why your heart's breath feels like it's gasping, panting, coughing, hiccupping, raspy, suppressed or obstructed?

Try breathing… *completely*!

Chapter 6

The Fool and the Prophet

My Heart, My Words

And Cain talked with Abel his brother: (Genesis 4:8a)

See to it that you do not refuse Him who is speaking. For if those did not escape when they refused him who warned them on earth, much less will we escape who turn away from Him who warns from heaven. (Hebrews 12:25 NASB)

The good man out of the good treasure of his heart brings forth what is good; and the evil man out of the evil treasure brings forth what is evil; for his mouth speaks from that which fills his heart. (Luke 6:45b NASB)

The Fool

Psalm 14:1 and 53:1 both reveal what is spoken in a fool's heart. His heart says, "*There is* no God." At first thought, the word *atheist* comes to mind. But more than merely claiming with their mouth that God does not exist, this person denies by their lifestyle that God is over them. Their innermost person or heart rejects that God is their superior and that He reigns and rules over all. They live out their days as if God isn't present and has no place in their daily affairs.

Other passages in the Bible give further description as to the characteristics of a fool. For instance, a fool plays a sport called mischief (Proverbs 10:23). A fool hates his father's instructions (Proverbs 15:5). He returns to his folly like a dog returns to his vomit (Proverbs 26:11).

Other passages link the word *fool* and the word *brutish* in the same verse, like Psalm 49:10 and Psalm 92:6. A brutish person can be described with words like "cruel," "absurd," "gross," "uncivilized," "animal-like," "irrational," "violent" and lacking understanding or human sense.

Some have even described a brutish person as one who makes such selfish choices that they are willing to put others at risk or danger. They may even hurt or kill a person. They are like a dangerous wild animal on the loose. Since a fool also lacks understanding and therefore makes poor choices that can affect others, we can see why these two are sometimes coupled in Scripture.

Continued examples and descriptions of foolish and brutish type people are found in the book of Jude. The book is written to believers of the church as a plea to "contend for the faith" (v.3). Jude, the brother of Jesus and James, is the author, though he identified himself as a *servant* of Jesus and a *brother* of James. In his letter he expresses a warning about ungodly men who were abusing the grace of God and denying Christ.

Jude wrote that those ungodly men spoke wickedly of the things they did not understand. These men were destruction to themselves because they spoke and lived out only what they knew naturally, like "brute beasts."

Jude goes on to list three examples whom the men in the church resembled: "Woe unto them! For they have gone in the way of Cain, and ran greedily after the error of Balaam for reward, and perished in the gainsaying of Core" (v.11).

Oh yes, this is *our* Cain; the one from Genesis 4. This, along with other descriptions of wickedness in the book of Jude, was what Cain was truly like. Just in case anyone tried to reason away or make excuses for Cain's wickedness, Jude reinforces the truth. Cain had played the part of a foolish brute. Jude describes the wickedness of the men in the church and they were compared to Cain.

As Jude continues, he describes these people as "spots in your feasts of charity, when they feast with you, feeding themselves without fear" (v.12a). "Spots" in this context means "blemishes." These people had no shame or respect. They abused the kindness of the host at his own table.

This is a reminder of Judas at the Last Supper who sat and ate with the Lord, yet was set to betray Him. It was said of Judas that Satan had entered into him and Jesus himself said about the twelve disciples, "one of you is a devil" (John 6:70). Judas was the *spot* at a meal of love. His betrayal came in the costume of a kiss.

Jude goes on to compare these ungodly church members to a few descriptive images. First, they are compared to clouds without water, meaning that they spoke promises they would never fulfill. Their words were empty. These same clouds get carried away by the wind because they are not rooted in godly doctrine or in God Himself.

They are also compared to rotting fruit on trees or trees with no fruit at all. Jude calls them "twice dead." This may mean they were dead once because of the sinful nature they were born into but dead twice as they have now chosen the path of eternal spiritual death; or perhaps Jude was showing a comparison between physical and spiritual death. All men die once physically, but some choose to die again spiritually by rejecting God.

Jude continued to describe these men in the church further with words like *wandering stars* and *raging waves of the sea,* etc. In verse 16, he said, "These are murmurers, complainers, walking after their own lusts; and their mouth speaketh swelling words, having men's persons in admiration because of advantage" (v.16).

In other words, they spoke in a way that they hoped would impress others or look good to them. The motive, of course, was to gain something from it, whether it be money, recognition or otherwise. The complaining and murmuring may have been under their breath, on the side or simply in their heart. Clearly, their motives were impure.

In light of all that Jude warned against, how do we interact with this kind of person? How do we converse with a person of this description? As we come back to Proverbs, two seemingly contradictory verses that are back-to-back speak about just that.

Proverbs 26:4-5 says, "Do not answer a fool according to his folly, or you will also be like him. Answer a fool as his folly deserves, that he not be wise in his own eyes" (NASB). Many have then asked, "Do I answer a fool or not answer him?" The answer is, "yes" to both and in the order they are written.

First, you should "not answer a fool" according to their folly. You can do this with careful consideration of the foundation from which a person is approaching you. A fool will approach you with an argument that is built on a worldly belief system. You will need to use discretion and make a mental separation. Truth will draw a dividing line between foundations. If you begin to debate them without using discernment, you become in danger of falling for their worldly doctrine. Before you know it, you are the one who is changing—and not for the better.

Galatians 6:1 reminds us, "Brethren, even if anyone is caught in any trespass, you who are spiritual, restore such a one in a spirit of gentleness; *each one* looking to yourself, so that you too will not be tempted" (NASB). Whether or not the person who is acting foolishly is saved, they need restoration. While helping them, we need to be careful that we do not fall for their way of life.

Before you are able to "answer a fool," you need to "not answer" him by using *judgment* about the situation. You need to discern the other person's beliefs and behaviors. Truth will keep your eyes enlightened and your feet on the right path.

Sometimes when people hear the word *judgment* in this (or any) context, they are quickly tempted to refer to Matthew 7 which tells us, "Do not judge so that you will not be judged" (v.1 NASB). We know that God is the ultimate Judge and that only He is the true discerner of hearts. However, Matthew 7 has more to its context than just this verse.

The commandment to "judge not" is to those (like the Pharisees) who judge as hypocrites. Just verses later, we are told that we can make a discernment and help our brother after we have removed the "log from our own eye."

We can help others well when we can see well. When we have spiritual vison, we can mentally separate our identity or behaviors from others. The result of this discernment will help us remain the person *we are* instead of becoming the person *they are*.

After "answering not a fool," you need to "answer a fool" so that he does not become wise in his own eyes. A few verses later, Proverbs 26:12 says, "Do you see a man wise in his own eyes? There is more hope for a fool than for him" (NASB).

A fool lacks understanding and therefore may be corrected with words of knowledge. Whether or not he takes that knowledge is up to him, but he has the opportunity to gain understanding. If he rejects it, he then moves closer to becoming a person wise in his own eyes.

A person *wise in their own eyes* is worse than a fool because this person believes they are truly wise. Their pride and haughty attitude will not allow for correction in their life. They think they are always right and have nothing to learn. In their own delusional estimation, they are better than anyone else. Pride and self-conceit have devoured them.

"Answering a fool" must become a strategic, verbal discrediting of their logic in order to provide an opportunity that can prevent them from becoming *wise in their own eyes.* It is to say something that will stop them in their tracks. Your words must shut down and discredit their arguments, which will provide a favorable moment for them to hear past their own voice. The "answer to a fool" has to be a statement that they cannot argue with and one that will give them the opportunity to have their eyes opened.

If we refer to the book of Jude again, we will see this whole process on *how to answer a fool* play out. In the midst of all that Jude is writing about to the Church, a seemingly arbitrary verse pops up. Verse nine says, "Yet Michael the archangel, when *contending* with the devil he *disputed* about the body of Moses, durst not bring against him a railing accusation, but said, 'The Lord rebuke thee'" (emphasis added).

We do not know what the dispute over Moses' body was about for certain. Ancient sources propose that Satan wanted Moses' body to be buried in a location where the Israelites would have access to his grave—that they might be tempted to worship it like a shrine. Some sources believe that Satan was bringing accusations against Moses in reference to his murder of an Egyptian and thus attempting some claim over his body.

Whatever the dispute was about, Jude's point is to teach us *how to answer a fool.* First, Jude uses the phrase "contending with the devil" (v.9). The word *contending* here is the Greek word *diakrino.*

> **Diakrino: "to distinguish, to judge." "I separate, distinguish, discern one thing from another; I doubt, hesitate, waver."**[19]

He next used the phrase "disputed about the body of Moses" (v.9). The word *disputed* is the Greek word *dialegomai.*

> **Dialegomai: "to discuss, to address, to preach."**[20]

HELPS Word-studies breaks the word down this way: dia, "through, from one side across to the other," and lego, "speaking to a conclusion."[21]

According to the same source, this Greek word "occurs 13 times in the NT, usually of believers exercising "dialectical reasoning." This is the process of giving and receiving information with someone to reach deeper understanding – a "going back-and-forth" of thoughts and ideas so people can better know the Lord (His word, will). Doing this is perhaps the most telling characteristic of the growing Christian!"[22]

The middle part of this word (*lego*) originally carried with it the idea of someone lying down to rest or sleep. This later carried over to the same concept concerning a dispute. It means to bring the dispute to a conclusion; putting it to rest.

All of this sounds a lot like the great advice from Proverbs and in the proper order. First we see that Michael will "not answer the fool" by intellectually distinguishing *(diakrino)* that he and the devil come from two separate foundations. The devil would like nothing more than to suck Michael into a debate that would entrap him and cause him to stumble. He would like nothing more than to get Michael's emotions riled up in hopes that it would cause him to slip from his firm foundation. However, Michael has drawn the line; he's made a separation. Clearly they are on opposing sides, as this is not Michael's first encounter with the devil.

Next, Michael will "answer a fool" by speaking a statement that is indisputable. The words, "The Lord rebuke you" must have stung worse than any other words Satan could have heard. Even though Satan is beyond being *wise in his own conceit* with simply no hope, Michael will speak words that bring the matter to a conclusion (*dialegomai*). He will let the power and authority of God bring judgment. It is His power alone that will defeat the devil and his wickedness.

Notice that Michael does not bring an accusation against Satan. Though Satan is guilty, as are many others that are controlled by him, accusations only make matters worse, for both parties. They certainly will not lead anyone towards the truth.

Michael seemingly did not carry on a lengthy

conversation with the devil. If the devil haunts you with his words of doubt, fear or chaos, bring the conversation to a close by letting him know who rules and reigns in your heart. Speak the name of the Lord Jesus Christ.

As we look to Genesis 4, we find out how this whole process regarding *how to answer a fool* played out in the life of Cain. First, God did "not answer the fool" in that He rejected Cain's offering.

When we think of Cain, we typically think of words like pride, anger, resistance, faithless and murderer. We are fully aware that Cain's foundation was not in God. So what was it in?

Cain's foundation was in Salvation by works. If Cain did not have the foundation of Salvation by works, he would have ignored God by not showing up at the offering scene at all. But Cain did show up and he actually approached God with an offering. It's that he approached with the wrong foundational belief—the foundation of himself.

Cain presented to God a display of the works of his own labor. He was trying to impress God and put on a show for those around him. Like the *swelling words* of the men Jude described, Cain was trying to look good on the outside in order to take advantage.

Notice also that Cain was among believers when he presented his offering. He was in the midst of the "church," so to speak. He participated in the "church practices" by presenting his offering. However, he too was like the *waterless clouds* that are all talk but no delivery.

After God "answered not a fool" by rejecting the foundation that Cain was approaching Him from, He then "answered the fool" by speaking words that discredited Cain's anger. "Why art thou wroth? and why is thy countenance fallen? If thou doest well, shalt thou not be accepted?" (Genesis 4:6-7a).

We already know that Cain's silence goes back to the *blank unrepentant stare* because he had tried to fool God in every way possible and had not succeeded. God had strategically spoken words that could not be disputed. He had discredited the fool by showing him that his anger was the result of his own choices. He was making it evident that Cain's sadness was produced by his disobedience. He was also proving that the steps were simple and that Cain had caused his own complications and chaos through his own wickedness.

Even though God rejected Cain's offering, He provided a brilliant series of questions which offered Cain the opportunity to see the truth.

> **The prudent wording of the wise offers healing (Proverbs 12:18).**

By discovering *how to answer a fool* through the interlocking passages from Proverbs, Psalms, Jude and Genesis, we can finally get to the text in Genesis 4:8a that states, "and Cain talked with Abel his brother."

In the light of what we just learned, we can more clearly picture what a last conversation between Cain and Abel may have looked like.

The Scene

When Genesis 4:8a says, "And Cain talked with Abel his brother," what exactly does this mean? Commentators differ on this short phrase. Some versions of the Bible have *added* an actual quote from Cain (not found in the original Hebrew text) which he spoke to Abel, that says, "Let's go out to the field." Commentators believe that this added statement from Cain (which was derived from the Septuagint and other ancient sources) indicates that Cain deceived Abel with kind words in order to trick him into going to the place where he could murder him. In other words, they believe Cain premeditated the murder.

Other commentators hold to the original Hebrew text of Genesis 4:8a, "And Cain talked with Abel his brother," (without additional words) and believe that this statement refers to Cain's conversation with Abel on the topic of the previous verses. They think that Cain spoke to Abel about what the Lord had spoken to Cain, which was the reason why his offering wasn't accepted as well as Satan's desire to overtake him. These commentators simply believe that Cain and Abel conversed before the murder.

To be fair, no one can account the actual details of how it all happened. Commentators are trying to fill in an obvious break in the text in order to aid readers with the flow and understanding of it. The verses go from God's admonition to Cain, to Cain talking with Abel; the next part of the verse states, "and it came to pass, when they were in the field, that Cain rose up against Abel his brother and killed him" (4:8b).

There is a third interpretation which combines both of the above interpretations. The Chaldee paraphrast (an Aramaic translation of the Old Testament) states that Cain did say, "Let's go out to the field" (with what initial intentions, we can't be certain), but adds that the brothers had a discourse in the field before the murder.

It is possible that Cain asked Abel to go to the field in order to have a private conversation with him—even if he had intentions to bully him. We can't be sure at which point Cain decided he would murder Abel. Cain's heart was wearing the kind of clothes that *could* lead to murder, but that doesn't mean he predetermined that it would go that far. Either way, his wild emotions had been stacked on top of the poor character he had already developed. The bottom line is, Cain made a deadly choice.

At some point Cain revealed all that was in his heart. Scripture tells us, "for his mouth speaks from that which fills his heart" (Luke 6:45b NASB). Often times people can get physically out of control (a fist in the wall, slamming of doors, etc.) after being fueled by their heated words. The angry *heart* produces matching *words* and angry *words* produce matching *actions*.

Recall that Jude described the wicked "church goers" as *raging waves* whose foam revealed their wickedness. You see, sin can only be held secret for so long, anger can only be bottled up for a time and deception can only be "controlled" while it is fresh. Eventually, there is no more ability to cover up who you really are. Eventually, the foam is revealed. There was no exception for Cain. At a certain moment in time, he could no longer pretend.

Like a pot of water on a stove, Cain's anger escalated right up to the boiling point of murder. I think he raised his *voice* to Abel and next, he raised his *hand*.

The Chaldee paraphrast adds that Cain declared to Abel words that disregarded the truth of God's identity. In turn, Abel declared to Cain the truth of who God was and the truth concerning future rewards for those who choose to follow Him and future consequences for those who choose to reject Him.

We cannot declare that this paraphrast has the weight of the original and inspired Hebrew text, nor can we be sure of all that happened leading up to the murder. However, we have already unraveled some truths about Cain's heart which reveal his disregard for God—and we are about to unravel some truths which confirm Abel's calling to speak of God's identity. This paraphrast simply seems to fit in with what we know (and will discover) about the hearts of these two brothers.

Based on what we know, let's take a look at a likely conversation between them and more importantly, how we should converse with the "Cain's" in our own life.

The Talk

In my experiences with other "Cain's," when issues are brought to a head, conversations usually boil down to the following: *false accusations, hatred and selfishness* and *fantasy worlds*.

False accusations - An accusatory person cannot admit their own wrongdoing. They become jealous of those who have a settled identity through Christ but are not willing to bend their knee to God to have one of their own. In these conversations, Satan uses the wicked to accuse the innocent of their own guilt. I believe Cain did just that.

Hate and selfishness - 1 Corinthians 13 tells us what love *does* and *does not* consist of: "Love is patient, love is kind *and* is not jealous; love does not brag *and* is not arrogant, does not act unbecomingly; it does not seek its own, is not provoked..." (vv. 4-5a NASB). All that love is *not* describes Cain to his core.

Proverbs 10:12a also reminds us that "hatred stirs up strife" (NASB). Perhaps Cain's words attempted to create friction between himself and Abel. This is why Cain's side of the conversation was likely so overheated. His words were also likely self-focused. He was a bragger—a show-off—a self-advertiser!

Fantasy world - As I have mentioned previously, I have dealt with many "Cain's" who have issues concerning time. I think Cain held onto bad memories of the past (some of which may never have been true). I think he spoke words of resentment toward Abel that reflected his incorrect perception of their childhood. I think Cain was living in the past and his words revealed his mental immaturity.

I also think he was living in a future world that didn't exist. He wanted to receive the favor of God but acted like he had already achieved it. He was mentally living in a world where he had already fooled God; where he *was* God. Pride caused him to mentally live in a future time that did not exist and never would occur!

Whatever Cain's exact issue, the cause arose from his refusal to surrender. He was *accusing* others of his own guilt, filling his heart with *hate* and *selfishness* and living in Satan's *fantasy world* instead of God's reality. Cain's heart was already dwelling in a far-off land.

Perhaps Cain spoke words like, "The Lord rejected my offering! But I did nothing wrong! I work hard every day to produce good fruit! No one knows how to grow and multiply seeds like I do. God doesn't know what He is talking about. He has no right to dictate *what* I should bring or *how* I should bring it. He's lucky He got anything at all. He has no appreciation for my work! Besides, no one could keep up with all of God's stupid rules anyway! And watch him try to judge me. I don't think so."

Perhaps the accusations turned towards Abel with, "You purposely tried to out-do me! You are always trying to get on God's good side and make me look bad. You've been doing this since we were kids. You used to always 'kiss up' to Mom and Dad. You'd always have to find the best flowers in the field to bring home to Mom and you'd always have to offer to help Dad when he was out in the fields working late—as if you were talented with produce. You always tried to make me look like the lazy one. I'm sick and tired of never being good enough for anyone when I'm better than all of you combined! All you and God want to do is interfere in my life! Not this time! I'm tired of you trying to correct and control me. You think you're so perfect. No longer! I'm not living in your shadow anymore! I am the firstborn and will not have that right taken away from me. It ends here and now!"

Why do I believe Cain spoke like this? It's because his *words* flowed from his *heart*. Cain was as spiritually dead as Abel was about to be physically dead. And spiritually dead people often speak words of death! **My Heart, My Words!**

On the other hand, Abel's words to Cain likely brought *truth, love* and *future warnings*.

In an exchange of words, Abel must have found that only *truth* could fight the lies and accusations of Cain. Abel did not get caught up in arguments or bunny trails that led to nowhere. Though he had no direct scriptures to quote, he simply stated the truths that God had implemented into his heart. I think he spoke the truth about who God was.

In addition to truth, perhaps Abel equally spoke words of *love*. Because Abel was wrapped up in who God was, he couldn't help but release love to others. Abel's words were not based on his brother's behavior. What his brother did and how he spoke would not change or dictate how Abel acted and responded. The love of God within Abel translated into a deep care about the soul and eternal destination of his brother.

Psalms 85:10 says, "Lovingkindness and truth have met together; righteousness and peace have kissed each other" (NASB). Through Abel's secure identity, he could deliver to Cain a balanced message of truth and love. For truth and love are not in opposition, but work together in perfect harmony.

> **Truth enlightens our eyes to see what is right and wrong and love compels us to choose what is right.**

Besides truth and love, perhaps Abel offered Cain a way to be pulled out of the fire. Proverbs 16:6 says, "By mercy and truth iniquity is purged: and by the fear of the Lord men depart from evil."

Near the end of Jude is a description of two ways in which godly believers lead others to Jesus: "And of some have compassion, making a difference: and others save with fear, pulling them out of the fire; hating even the garment spotted by the flesh" (vv. 22-23). Cain was way beyond being influenced by compassion. He rebelled against the godly examples in his life, he resisted the compassion and advice from the Lord and he quenched any amount of conviction in his heart.

Knowing Cain's opposition, perhaps Abel attempted to save him through fear; through *future warnings*. Perhaps he made a last attempt at telling Cain about the terror of the Lord if he did not turn around now.

Abel was not too prideful to remember that he was once "foolish, disobedient, deceived, serving divers lusts and pleasures, living in malice and envy, hateful *and* hating one another" (Titus 3:3). There was a time when he had to remove the clothes that Jude describes as a "spotted garment."

This was why it wasn't Cain that Abel hated but rather, his clothing. I think Abel's cry was for Cain to take the garment off. I can almost hear Abel pour out his heart to his brother. I think he mustered up every ounce of energy that he could and gave Cain what a powerful preacher would give if he knew he were delivering his last sermon on earth.

I think he was *broken* for his brother, *bold* in his speech and *brave* because of his confidence in God. I'm quite assured that Abel witnessed to Cain—and likely, this was not the first time.

"Cain… there is no one greater than God. He is Alpha and you know He cannot be overcome. He created you for His glory and He has a plan for your life which will give you fulfillment and joy. Look at the person that you've become. Is this what you want? Surrender to the One who created you in His image. His everlasting love can renew you. He has been patiently waiting for you fall into His open arms. There is mercy and rest there. His laws have shown you where you err so you will recognize that you need Him. You need Him to be the good that you lack. Take it off, Cain! Surrender so that your anger and wickedness can come off and God can put His goodness on you. Trust in His promise of a Seed that will redeem you! Have faith in the One who loves you. Believe in the One who has an abundant and eternal life for you. Confess your sins. Do it now before His judgments pour out on you! Walk His mercy bridge so that you may escape the punishment that you deserve! Two roads diverge before you, Cain. Take the one that ends with a win! Take the one that defeats death and offers you life!"

Do you see what Abel did? Like a parent teaching a child, Abel showed Cain how to play "connect the dots." Abel just drew a picture whose first dot was first letter of the Greek Alphabet, Alpha, and whose last dot was the last letter, Omega. In between were the dots of all the attributes, names and descriptions of who God is. When Abel was done connecting the dots, the picture of God's all-encompassing identity was revealed. Perhaps the picture looked much like a giant heart.

After Abel created this picture, possibly he brought the conversation back to the process of "not answering a fool" and "answering a fool." When it came to "not answering a fool," I believe Abel had already drawn the line between right and wrong—which made it possible for him to keep his godly character and remain unaffected by his brother's poor behavior. I'm sure it was quite clear to Abel that he and his brother came from two different foundations. I think Abel predetermined that he would not be swayed from his strong faith in God.

As Abel had tried to reach his brother over the years and only received resistance from him, perhaps he had come to the point where he needed to "answer the fool" by speaking words that drew a conclusion and could not be debated.

Quite possibly with passion and tears, Abel said something like, "Cain, is there not a gaping hole within you? If you give yourself to God completely, will He not complete you? If you take off those filthy rags, will He not cover you with His beautiful robe? If you lay your heart on the altar, will He not rescue it from consuming flames?"

Why do I think this? Why do I believe Abel spoke like this? It's because his *words* flowed from his *heart*. **My Heart, My Words!** Jesus, in Luke 11:50-51, revealed that Abel had lived out a calling that went far beyond his occupation of shepherd. Abel, rather, had an identity that was totally enveloped in who God was—and because of it, he fulfilled the calling of who God had designed him to be.

Abel was—a prophet.

In Luke eleven, Jesus had spoken with some of the experts of the law (lawyers) and he pointed out their hypocritical ways of saying or doing things that looked good, while their hearts and intents were wicked. In their hearts they had taken part of what their ancestors had done; which was the murdering of the prophets. Surely some of them would take part in the death of Jesus as well.

Because of their hypocrisy, Jesus said that "the blood of all the prophets, shed since the foundation of the world, may be charged against this generation, from the blood of Abel to the blood of Zechariah" (Luke 11:50-51a NASB).

As Cain's life was much like these hypocritical lawyers, Abel's death was much like the bloodshed of our Lord. He was a prophet who foreshadowed the True Prophet to come.

The Prophet

A prophet is simply one who calls others to repentance. They are also known to admonish, rebuke and warn others of the judgment they will face if they do not renounce their sins. They may also interpret Scripture, predict or see things afar off.

1 Samuel 9:9 says, "(Beforetime in Israel, when a man went to inquire of God, thus he spake, Come, and let us go to the seer: for *he that is now called* a Prophet was beforetime called a Seer.)" We already know that those in Hebrews 11 saw things afar off and Abel is listed among them. He is a seer. And here, he saw that his brother was headed for fire!

Today, as New Testament believers, the Bible is clear that the Holy Spirit gives us all different gifts such as teaching, serving, giving, mercy and yes, prophecy.

A person with this gift has much discernment when interacting with others. They are aware of the deeper meanings in life. They can detect the root of evil because they have definitively drawn the lines between right and wrong. They can draw those lines because they can *see* the consequence or reward down the road. They also have a strong desire for truth and are willing to suffer for the sake of Christ.

This was Abel. I don't think that he was oblivious to the fact that he could undergo adversity for the sake of God. Jesus tells us in Luke 4:24 that "No prophet is accepted in his own country." Jesus knew that His own people and even some of His own family members (for a time) would refuse to accept His true identity and yet He suffered the rejection anyway.

Quite possibly, Abel knew it too. Perhaps (before talking with Cain) Abel knew there was a good chance that Cain would reject the truth yet he pressed forward with living out his true calling and identity anyway. Although Cain physically killed Abel, perhaps it was Abel who lay down his life willingly for Cain. As a shepherd, Abel knew how to love and care for his sheep. He may have known the concept of John 15:13, "Greater love has no one than this, that one lay down his life for his friends" (NASB).

Perhaps Abel knew there was something greater than words. Perhaps he knew that actions could speak far more than his lips could express. Perhaps he knew there was no greater act that could influence sinners to repent than a sacrificial act of love. Perhaps Abel gave up all of his rights for the cause of his Redeemer—even the right to live!

Could Abel have foreshadowed Jesus by laying down his life? Romans chapter five tells us that it would be rare if a man died for someone who was righteous, yet Jesus died for the unrighteous (vv.5-6). Did Abel resemble Jesus in this way? Did he willingly face the possibility of death to give Cain one more opportunity for repentance?

I'm not sure if Abel could actually foresee his own murder but I believe that he had no fear, because he was already "sold out" no matter the cost! He would live for God until the day that he gained an eternity with Him (Philippians 1:21).

If you have the gift of prophecy, *take note* that those closest to you may refuse to accept the message that your life and lips deliver. But *take heart* because as far as you can foresee, God can foresee much further! Your temporary rejection may be a part of a much bigger plan of eternal redemption. Continue to live out your true identity and calling whatever you face!

As for Abel, everything about him was handed over to God, including his specific gift of prophecy. He did not abuse it. In fact, I think he used it as God would have him to right up until his last earthly words. His life and even his death *predicted* a future story that was set to change eternity!

Perhaps you are an "Abel" who has surrendered but you have a "Cain" in your life that has not. This may be a person who has never come to know Christ as their Savior like Cain or it may be someone who is saved but "Cain-like" characteristics keep rising up within them. Maybe it's a child, or sibling or even a spouse or parent.

It's not always easy to know how to effectively interact with or reach out to them but I'd encourage you to keep two words in mind: *discretion* and *reflection*. Use *discretion* to draw the lines so that you do not become like them. Use a mirror as *reflection* to help them see the ridiculous costume they have on. Whatever the situation, the *heart of it* is to challenge the core of their inner thoughts in order to give them an opportunity to see the light.

This challenge must contain love or all efforts will be in vain. In fact, without love, you are like the ear-splitting noise of two cymbals banging together (1 Corinthians 13:1). There is no feeling of heart and soul behind that music.

Without love, the gift of prophecy and the kind of faith that is required to see miracles will not fulfill the purpose of who God designed you to be. Without love, giving to the poor and sacrificing your body will not secure you a benefit (1 Corinthians 13:2-3). There must be love! For, God *is* love.

Putting sincere love behind your actions, words and tone will not guarantee a positive outcome. It certainly didn't in the life of Cain. However, it does provide the *opportunity* for a person to surrender and become renewed. This is exactly what Jesus provided through his love act on the cross—an offer of renewal and an opportunity for eternal life.

How you converse with a person is based on your purpose. Is your purpose to force them into a robotic march of compliance or is it to see their heart renewed into the person God created them to be?

> **The intent to influence the heart-change of another, should be driven from the heart-change that's already happened in you!**

Speak truth. Speak love. Speak God's identity.

Chapter 7

Killer or Keeper

My Heart, My Actions

> and it came to pass, when they were in the field, that Cain rose up against Abel his brother, and slew him. And the LORD said unto Cain, Where is Abel thy brother? And he said, I know not: Am I my brother's keeper? (Genesis 4:8b-9)

> 'YOU SHALL LOVE YOUR NEIGHBOR AS YOURSELF.' (Mark 12:31 NASB)

The Wrong Blood

Genesis 4:8b states that "when they were in the field, that Cain rose up against Abel his brother, and slew him."

I can't help but wonder what field this was. Was Abel out walking the sheep field fulfilling his daily chores? Did this happen in Cain's crop territory? Maybe it was where the two fields met by a brook where the brothers would take a water break. Whatever the case and whenever this occurred, it was in Cain's heart to eliminate his brother.

1 John 3:12 reveals why Cain killed his brother by saying, "Not as Cain, *who* was of that wicked one, and slew his brother. And wherefore slew he him? Because his own works were evil, and his brother's righteous." Cain was evil *before* the murder! Bloodshed has a prerequisite—evil works.

John continues to say, "Everyone who hates his brother is a murderer" (1 John 3:15a NASB). There is a progression that occurred in Cain that is a warning to us all. Hate murders people in *heart* and can often lead to murder in *body*. We can then ask, "what kind of things lead to hate?"

Just two verses later, John says, "But whoso hath this world's good, and seeth his brother have need, and shutteth up his bowels of compassion from him, how dwelleth the love of God in him?" (v.17). We often view hate as some extreme act in order to give reason as to why we are not guilty of it. John says it can start by losing our compassion for people who are in need.

Even after having learned the "why" of Cain's murder of his brother, I still find myself wondering "how." How could he do it? How could he actually go through with it?

My brother, who is about two and a half years older than I, is the "smart one". Growing up, he could read a book or any academic material and take a test without hardly any, if any, studying. He was witty and could dream up a comeback for everything. His passion was (and still is) music, and in fact, many times his comebacks were sung to me in perfect rhythm and rhyme, all off the top of his head. He was too smart.

As kids, we often fought over the dumbest things. There were days that he drove me to insanity. If we were ever punished to our bedrooms, my brother would whisper to me from his room across the hall. He would say, "Come on.

Let's say we're sorry so we can get out of our rooms." This drove me even further! I wanted him to suffer and beg for mercy. I was so serious about it and my brother was so lighthearted and whimsical.

It wasn't that he wasn't sorry, but that he had already put it behind him. He had moved on. I, on the other hand, was stubborn and wanted the upper hand for a change. However, as my brother continued to whisper across the hall, my heart would eventually melt. After all, he was my brother. He could always get me to smile, calm down and see things another way. In the end, we were both sorry and ready to start over.

I propose again, how could Cain kill his brother? Because the story of Cain and Abel is only one chapter long and the murder is narrated in only one of those verses, it can be easy to move past it by just chalking-it-up to "the first murder." If it doesn't affect our present and personal life, this verse can be quickly dismissed from our mind. If we take some time and place ourselves in the moment, in someone else's shoes, we walk away with a deeper reality of what really occurred.

Cain literally killed his brother with his own hands (Genesis 4:11). Exactly how, we do not know, but there was a moment when Abel breathed his last earthly breath. Blood was spilt. The snap shot image of Abel's dead body lying on the ground as his blood seeped into the earth must have troubled Cain for many years to come.

Cain's heart was likely racing and his anger overflowing. Quite possibly his hands were shaking or even covered in Abel's blood. Perhaps he was sweating from the physical struggle to overpower his brother. Maybe he stood there for a moment as a statue in total shock. Perhaps he enjoyed the feeling of power and victory. Perhaps he ran as to not be spotted at the crime scene or to uphold his alibi in another field. Did he perchance wash up at a nearby stream or attempt to dispose of any other evidence that could implicate him?

Either way, this was no accident. At some point, it became the clear intention in Cain's heart to murder Abel. Cain became like a wild animal with no regard for its prey. His murder of Abel was without cause, and pleading "Not Guilty" for reason of insanity was not an option. In fact, the next several verses will show that Cain was not insane because he attempted to hide his crime through a lie. He also later whined about his punishment after knowing he was caught. Cain clearly knew right from wrong—he just chose the wrong.

Any level of mental illness that Cain had was a direct result from his own choices that allowed Satan to have a foothold into his mind. Every decision along the way gave Satan more control. Cain chose to be *under the influence* of Satan!

He literally did the opposite of what he should have. He *did* bring a fruit offering but he did *not* produce fruit spiritually. He did *not* bring a blood offering, but he *did* produce blood physically! It was the wrong fruit *and* the wrong blood!

It was also in the wrong order. If Cain had produced a blood offering through faith *first,* he would have naturally produced spiritual fruit *second.*

The humble heart is desperate for the blood of Christ.

The loving heart is willing to sacrifice the blood of itself.

The prideful heart demands and steals the blood of others!

Brother's Keeper

Sometime after Cain killed his brother and likely had fled the scene, the Lord said to him, "Where is Abel your brother?" (Genesis 4:9 NASB). The Lord didn't ask this because He didn't know the answer, but rather, He was giving Cain a chance to confess his crime.

Also, consider that the Lord called Abel "his brother." Cain certainly knew who Abel was. However, he had disregarded how one should treat one's brother. The Lord used this simple phrase to bring light and truth to the topic of identity.

Cain's first part of his reply was, "I know not" (v.9). This response was, of course, no more than a lie. Cain had already murdered, in addition to other sins that contributed to his wickedness. I can only imagine that lying was a natural first response for him. A lying tongue is listed among six things that the Lord hates in Proverbs 6. In fact, the first three in that list of six are, "A proud look, a lying tongue, and hands that shed innocent blood" (v.17). It's a perfect description of Cain.

In addition to lying, Cain's pride pushed forward as his tongue released a "dig" in the form of a question, "Am I my brother's keeper?" (Genesis 4:9).

It is interesting that just as the Lord released light on the topic of identity, Cain brought darkness as he mocked God with the very same topic. "Am I my brother's keeper?" has a few different meanings.

First, it was spoken in **pride**. The word *keeper* here means "to keep, watch, preserve"[23]. Remember that Abel was a "keeper of sheep." Abel's job was to *preserve* and tend to what was already living.

Cain was a "tiller of the ground" and his job was to grow and produce. His job was creative in the sense that the sprouting, blooming and growing of seeds, plants and trees was a process in which Cain may have felt he had direct control over the outcome.

Cain was laboriously "creating" something while Abel was caring for and preserving what was already created. Obviously what Cain was growing was once created too but as he used his creativity to produced more of it, his hands and heart turned prideful with the results from his labor.

It's good to be creative. The creativity within us is directly from God. The problem really arises when we forget that. Pride moves us to lose sight that we are the result of His creativity and that the good that flows from us is due to what *first* flowed from Him.

There was, of course, a *tending* part to Cain's job just as there was *creativity* in Abel's preservation job. However, the preservation part of Cain's job did not cater to the temporary high he acquired from creating something new. Cain's heart echoed discontentment. He endlessly longed for the next new thing to fill up his heart's void.

Living everyday life as a steady and faithful shepherd (as Abel did) would never have been appealing to Cain. It wasn't exciting enough. It didn't give him the spike of flashy accomplishment. Although there can be creativity in preservation, Cain desired production and results that heightened his ego.

I'm concerned that we are no different. We want the next new thing because what we already have is unsatisfying to preserve. Our problem lies deep within our hearts!

I can almost hear Cain thinking about or mockingly saying to Abel, "Look what I created today! See the amazing results of my talented hands? What did you do today? Oh... that's right! You tended a flock of sheep."

In today's world, we have husbands that come home (to their wives; keepers of the children) from their creative and laborious jobs bragging about all of their accomplishments and looking for applause with an attitude that says, "What I do is more important than what you do."

Perhaps, rather, it's a mother who is unsatisfied with caring for her children as if the job isn't creative enough. She is tired of being surrounded by the same four walls with the same four needy kids. She has lost sight that the reward of her preservation is just a bit further down the road (Galatians 6:9).

In other scenarios, there are missionaries, pastors or others in full time ministry who have become so focused on the results of their creative labor that they have forgotten about preserving and tending to their family.

In marriages, there are spouses who would rather strike up a new relationship with someone else instead of preserving their current union.

In the daily grind, instead of cleaning our homes, taking care of our belongings, paying our bills and fulfilling our responsibilities, we have decided it would be more exhilarating to do and have "the new."

At some point though, we are forced to do something about what has been long neglected. We end up throwing out or wasting what was improperly used or overly abused. We end up in debt or some situation that requires our savings (which was long spent by a thrill here and there). Frustration is at its peak as if someone else is at fault for the long overlooked messy house we live in.

In general, our culture has turned toward what is instant and thrilling and away from what is faithful and responsible.

If we could forget about the flashy, if we could set aside our selfishness and stop the prideful attempts of showing off our good works and labor, if we could let go of the temporary highs that do not satisfy our souls, could we not simply use our creativity in the everyday life moments? Could we not be "our brother's keeper" with imagination and inventiveness? Could we not be artistic and inspirational towards those we are preserving?

> **In your creativity, don't forget about preserving what was already created! In your preservation, don't forget to use your creativity!**

In God's identity, we find this balance. He is both the Creator of us and the Keeper of us. He did not dismiss His creation after sin but provided a creative way to keep it!

As for Cain, he had an attitude that acted like being a "keeper of his brother" was beneath him. He was a creator of the new, not a preserver of the old. He was growing and producing his own identity and his pride would not allow others to interrupt his creative flow!

Cain's famous "brother's keeper" question was not only spoken in pride but spoken to declare his **title**. Cain was curling up his lip at the thought of "brother's keeper" being his title. He had a title in mind that recognized and elevated himself, not one that lifted up his brother.

He spoke his question in a way that indicated he had a much better title than the one he believed God was imposing on him. I can hear him thinking, "I am Cain, the firstborn son of the world. I am the best tiller of the ground. I work and run this land. Look at the results of my long hours of labor. I don't have the time to be the keeper of Abel."

It's as if Cain was attempting to prove who he was by referring to the results of his work. It was as if the substance of his identity was tied to his success and position. It was as if he believed "keeping his brother" conflicted with his high and mighty status.

Not only was Cain working in a field near Abel, but they were brothers of the same family. Though their connection was two-fold, Cain was asking if he was his brother's keeper as if God had changed his job description or added to his responsibilities.

In reality, Cain had changed his own job description. He had added to it the title of "killer." The man who apparently had no time to *keep*, somehow had plenty of time to *kill*.

Being his "brother's keeper" should have been a part of who Cain was every day. "Brother's Keeper" should have been factored into his thoughts and time. He just never wanted it to be. He just never fulfilled the role of the person God had for him to become. Instead, he neglected any care or love for his brother as he sought a more famous title.

Cain's main problem stemmed from his refusal of the most important title of all; Child of God. A child of God concerns himself with the matters of God. And God is all about His creation. God is all about love. God is all about people. If you're too important for people, God is not too important to you.

A lover of God is a keeper of man!

Whatever job you're in or whatever title you have, God will place before you "brother's keeper moments." These moments are clear because the purpose of them is the same purpose you were made for: bringing glory to God moment by moment in everyday life. Your job is not separate from your keeping. Your true inner and eternal title must be present at the place of your earthly title. The real "you" must show up to work. The real "you" must always be ready for a keeping moment no matter where you are or what you're doing.

It was midnight and my phone rang. It was a call from my co-worker (and friend) who had been facing some tough life circumstances. He was stranded at the hospital and needed transportation. Beyond that night, the next several months consisted of days where I received a 5:00 a.m. phone call to cover his early morning work shift. On the days he was able to emotionally, mentally and physically make it to work, there were often "brother's keeper moments" that took place through raw conversation, a lot of listening and more often than not, buckets of tears.

It was 2:00 a.m. another time, when I got a call from a student who was stranded in the "bricks" (one of the most dangerous parts of the city). This kid had messed up big time and became afraid for his life. No one had known where he was and he had no one else to call on for a rescue. This "brother's keeper moment" was tag-teamed with my mom.

Sometimes our keeper moments may be helping an elderly neighbor carry in her groceries. It may be wiping the snow off the car next to you in some car lot. It may be a smile or an encouraging word to a cashier. It may be a hug, some tears and a silent moment between friends. It may be behavioral correction to your child. It may be a meal for a friend who just had a baby. Perhaps it's a prayer for someone God has brought to your mind.

When we "sign up" to love God, we "sign up" to love people. Maybe we have forgotten that we are called to **edify** (Romans 14:19), **exhort** (Hebrews 3:13), **warn, comfort, support, have patience** (1 Thessalonians 5:14), **consider** (Hebrews 10:24), **forgive** (Ephesians 4:32), **bear** (Galatians

6:2), **serve** (Galatians 5:13), **pray** (James 5:16) and **love** (John 13:34). Look at the responsibility we have toward humankind. This is how we keep!

Are you your brother's keeper? Or do you portray a careless attitude toward others? Do you act like you are better than others? Do you come across as self-centered or unapproachable? Have you cut yourself off from those in need? Have you surrounded yourself with only those whom you hope will never have to call on you? Do you ignore the needs of the public around you? Do you even notice their needs? Or are you so tied up in your own world and your own agenda that you are barely aware of those who are within your view, your reach?

The bigger question is, do those who already know you, believe you to be a keeper? Do people know before a situation happens to them that you are your brother's keeper? Do they already know ahead of time that you are a light, shelter and a rescue from the storm? Do they know they can call on you? Or are others such an inconvenience to you that no one would even consider calling on you for a situation that required care, concern, advice or service?

I think Cain's attitudes over the years proved to Abel that he could not call on his brother in a situation that required sincere and tender care. Cain's title, his work and his outward image were far more important to him.

Oh sure, Cain knew exactly where his brother was—but not because he loved him. What he knew was the place where he had left his brother's motionless body!

In addition to pride and title, Cain's famous "brother's keeper" question was spoken with a **twist**. Perhaps Cain's question was a mockery to God in the sense that he was asking, "Isn't that Your job, God? Like Abel is a keeper of sheep, aren't You supposed to be the keeper of him? That's what he tells me, anyway. If You're God, don't You know where he is? Or did You neglect to fulfill Your duties? Why are You trying to pin Your keeper job on me?" In his heart, Cain may have thought, "You obviously aren't a good keeper if you couldn't stop me from killing him!"

Enough said here. Cain's thoughts are clearly twisted.

Lastly, Cain's famous brother's keeper question was spoken as an **accusatory trap**. Back in the retail world, as a manager, I often had to rework schedules or move employees around into other departments to cover the needs of the business. It was always made known to employees that they were expected to be flexible and willing to do whatever was needed on any given day. Apparel employees were cross-trained to ring at the register, and golf specialists were trained in exercise and sports equipment. We were a team trained to use all of our skills and knowledge to assist the store as a greater whole.

One particular Cain-like associate did not like to be bothered or moved from his department. The situation developed to the point that other managers gave in to that person so they didn't have to deal with his attitude or complaints. This partiality became a problem. Other employees had to be flexible while this employee was given allowance, even if the business needs demanded otherwise.

On a particular day, I made the decision to move this employee from his department to cover a half hour break for another associate in footwear (a department in which he was highly knowledgeable). Let's just say he was not a team player. I was questioned just like God, "Am I a footwear sales associate?" What came next was an end result much similar to Cain's.

"Am I my brother's keeper?" was spoken as an accusatory *trap*. It's almost as if Cain was close to slipping up when he spoke his question. What he may have thought in his head was, "Am I my brother's killer? I mean, keeper?" Cain was feeling accused but only because he was guilty. I think Cain attempted to try turning the tables by making God look guilty no matter how He answered his "brother's keeper" question.

If God had answered "No," then Cain might have said, "Then why are You asking me? I'll be getting back to my hard work now. Good luck." To cover up his own guilt, Cain would have attempted to make God look guilty for interrupting his important laborious duties.

If God had said "yes," then Cain might have said, "You never told me that Abel was a part of my responsibility. You need to be clearer about what you expect from me. If I take on that responsibility, what other one would You like me to give up? I can't do everything!" To cover up his guilt in this scenario, Cain would have attempted to make God look guilty of adding too much to his workload or of having poor manager and communication skills.

Cain wanted God to be wrong no matter how He answered his question. Like the Pharisees who had set a trap with the purpose of accusing Jesus when they brought before Him an adulterous woman (John 8:6), Cain set the trap to accuse God. Of course, it didn't work!

The Threat of Losing

Most of us believe that we would never physically kill someone. But did you know that the consuming desire to gain can put you in a vulnerable position for murder to take place? Look at this verse in James… "You lust and do not have; so you commit murder. You are envious and cannot obtain; so you fight and quarrel. You do not have because you do not ask" (James 4:2 NASB).

If we're not asking or seeking God—with the right intent (James 4:3), we will not gain the good things that God has for us. When we cannot obtain what *we* want, we feel envious and take action to fight. Even murder can take place when we don't get what we lusted after. It all comes back to our treasure. Murder can occur by seeking the wrong treasure or by seeking any treasure without seeking God.

Certainly Cain had an earthly treasure in his heart. The threat of losing his *treasure* moved him to *do* whatever it took to preserve the life of his pride, title and confidence (as false as it was). Nothing was off the table if it meant Cain could *gain* and *keep* what he wanted—not even murder! **My Heart, My Actions!**

What if we surrendered to God all that we can't keep (earthly treasure) and trusted Him with what He promises we can never lose (heavenly treasure)? Somehow I think we'd be a better keeper of our brother if we did!

Chapter 8

Identity Swap

Surrender the Old, Receive the New

And he said, What hast thou done? the voice of thy brother's blood crieth unto me from the ground. And now art thou cursed from the earth, which hath opened her mouth to receive thy brother's blood from thy hand; When thou tillest the ground, it shall not henceforth yield unto thee her strength; a fugitive and a vagabond shalt thou be in the earth. And Cain said unto the LORD, My punishment is greater than I can bear. Behold, thou hast driven me out this day from the face of the earth; and from thy face shall I be hid; and I shall be a fugitive and a vagabond in the earth; and it shall come to pass, that every one that findeth me shall slay me. And the LORD said unto him, Therefore whosoever slayeth Cain, vengeance shall be taken on him sevenfold. And the LORD set a

> mark upon Cain, lest any finding him should kill him. (Genesis 4:10-15)
>
> And ye are complete in him. (Colossians 2:10a)

The Punishment

After Cain refused to admit his crime and spoke his "brother's keeper" question, the Lord said to Cain, "What hast thou done?" (Genesis 4:10a). It's like when a parent discovers crayon markings all over the living room wall. They say to their child, "What did you do?!?!?" It's not that the parent doesn't know *what* the child did. It's that the parent is pointing out the naughtiness. They are not asking *if* they did it. They are declaring the guilt. God knew what Cain had done to Abel!

Remember how Cain had spoken his "brother's keeper" question as a trap? Of course, God did not fall for it. Instead, He answered Cain by following the pattern of "not answering and answering a fool." He had no reply to Cain's direct question because He separated Himself from the false foundation from which Cain was addressing Him. Instead, He moved on to "answering" Cain by distributing the punishment, which brought the matter to a conclusion.

The Lord said, "And now art thou cursed from the earth, which hath opened her mouth to receive thy brother's blood from thy hand; When thou tillest the ground, it shall not henceforth yield unto thee her strength; a fugitive and a vagabond shalt thou be in the earth" (Genesis 4:11-12). Cain's occupational dreams of continuing to produce fruit from the ground were over. The dirt that he once thought he had so much control over would now decline his endeavors.

Herein lies more proof of the sovereignty of God over His creation.

Cain also became a wanderer (fugitive) in the earth. How ever that looked physically, it was due to his wandering spiritually. Proverbs 21:16 reminds us, "A man who wanders from the way of understanding will rest in the assembly of the dead" (NASB). This wandering identity is the one who refuses to repent. Spiritual and eternal death is the result. Recall that Jude compared this kind of man to a "wandering star."

Just moments ago, Cain was accusing God of *adding* to his responsibilities. In a swift turn of events, because Cain had abused his responsibilities, privileges and even his family, he would be taken away from it all; a *subtracting* of sorts. The ground would reject his efforts, any rights of being firstborn or benefits of living on that land had been removed and his relationship with his parents had been severed.

Cain was uprooted from it all. His pride in his identity was surely "squashed"—or rather, the stock that he placed his identity in, was "squashable" material.

The Mark

I can only imagine that Adam and Eve and their other children must have felt a whole host of emotions upon hearing that Cain had murdered Abel. Proverbs 17:25 says, "A foolish son *is* grief to his father, and bitterness to her that bare him." Oh, how Adam and Eve must have felt that sorrow! They were losing their first two children.

Did they feel guilt over how they raised Cain? Did they feel exhausted from all the efforts they made in showing him a right and godly way of life? Did they feel like failures? Did they replay past incidents in their heads which were all signs leading up to this horrific event? Did they feel like they hadn't protected Abel? What went through their minds as they found out their one son was a murderer and the other was dead?

Cain was not the only one losing here. Abel lost his life, Adam and Eve lost both Cain and Abel and the other children lost their older two brothers. The choice of one man affected so many. Pain, hurt and many questions must have overshadowed them.

This murderous event brought with it another moment of needed surrender on the family's part. Instead of seeking out their own way to punish Cain, they needed to let the Almighty take vengeance and focus on their own healing and forgiveness.

Cain would have to face God on his own. After he received his punishment, though, he whined about it, saying, "my punishment *is* greater than I can bear. Behold, thou hast driven me out this day from the face of the earth; and from thy face shall I be hid; and I shall be a fugitive and a vagabond in the earth; and it shall come to pass, *that* every one that findeth me shall slay me" (vv.13-14). Can you hear the pitiful tone in his voice? Now that he was getting punished, Cain suddenly had a lot to say.

This verse indicates that there were more people on earth than we may have realized. There are more descendants of Adam and Eve—and Cain knows that his actions may have caused at least one of these family members to want to kill him and take revenge for Abel's sake.

After Cain's complaint, the Lord declared that whoever killed Cain would suffer vengeance sevenfold. He then set a mark on Cain that would be an indicator and deterrent to anyone who desired to kill him. However, neither Cain's whining nor the mark changed his punishment.

Although many have proposed differing ideas about

what the mark (or sign) actually was or looked like, it is really more about what the mark indicated. I think the mark on Cain was an indicator of four things:

First, it **preserved** him (temporarily). Although Cain did not preserve his brother, God spared Cain from immediate termination.

This kind of preservation was written about by David in Psalm 59 when he was spied on by King Saul's men who had intentions to kill him. Verse 11 says, "Do not slay them, or my people will forget; Scatter them by Your power, and bring them down, O Lord, our shield!" (NASB). David was *not* asking for his enemy to be immediately and utterly destroyed. He was asking to for them to be scattered or (as we can relate in Genesis) to make them be as *wanderers.*

The purpose of David's request was so that his people would not forget. Though the passage doesn't specifically say what they should have remembered, we know that enemy presence can often make God's people look to Him and trust Him completely.

The enemies' *wandering* would give David and his men immediate relief. However, the *preservation* of their life would display a physical reminder for David and his people to remain faithful instead of following after their wicked ways.

Perhaps (at times) David was a preservationist toward the wicked physically so that he could preserve God's people spiritually. After all, David was once a "keeper of sheep". He knew a lot about preservation.

In the same way, perhaps God had a purpose for preserving Cain that would aid His people to draw clear lines in distinguishing their identity from their enemies. Could the temporary preservation of Cain's life have promoted spiritual preservation for God's people?

Perhaps there is bigger picture that our human insights and demands don't always comprehend. What if we could just trust God and remain faithful instead of relying on our *own understanding* (Proverbs 3:5)?

Secondly, even though the mark temporarily preserved Cain, it also eternally **reserved** him. We saw how Jude compared the ungodly men within the church of his time to three men, one of whom is Cain. Jude also described three situations in which God's judgment is viewed through the lens of *preservation and reservation.*

First, Jude recalls that the Lord saved people out of Egypt but later He destroyed those who did not believe (v.5). The second example was of the angels who were once preserved in heaven but left their home to be reserved for chains, darkness and judgment (v.6). The third example was the cities of Sodom and Gomorrah. These people defiled the flesh and committed fornication. They were stated as a lesson of who not to become. They would suffer in eternal flames forever (v.7).

These three groups were *preserved* for a time and purpose but they had been eternally *reserved* in the worst kind of way and by their own choice.

Cain was facing life without parole both temporarily and eternally. This was a permanent sentence based on the permanent choice that he made—not the choice of murder (because no single sin nor any amount of sins are unforgivable), but the choice of rejecting God's convictions, withholding a cry of confession and refusing his heart's surrender.

The mark spoke of the person Cain had decided to become forever—one apart from God. To choose to be apart from God is to choose the reservation of utter terror and torment. Cain was given ample opportunity to change his reservation and he refused.

When we consider that Cain's mark of reservation was placed on him before the end of his life, let's not forget that God is a just God. His knowledge is beyond our understanding and therefore He can judge in a far greater capacity. The future is not unknown to Him. In the case of Cain, the righteous Judge placed a reservation on him because He already knew what Cain had forever chosen in his heart.

In the case of you, if there is any amount of conviction within yourself, it is not too late to accept God's everlasting invitation and preservation. The grace of God is ready to pour out over any sinner who will repent!

Thirdly, the mark **proclaimed** *God's title* of judge and avenger. The mark was a declaration that man should not take action into his own hands. I think this applied to both anyone desiring to kill Cain as well as Cain's actions that killed Abel. Cain had declared his own elevated sense of identity over and over until it came crashing down. God's declaration of His title as Judge proved to Cain and others that His identity will never crash down. Even though Cain refused to surrender to God, his whining about the punishment proved that he knew he could not escape the Judge.

A criminal in today's age can lie all they want. They can even bring up all kinds of (brother's keeper) questions in an attempt to blame others. But when the judge or jury finds them guilty, the criminal realizes that punishment is unavoidable, and therefore the only thing left to do is whine and plead.

This is a reminder that regardless of man's ability to have free-will in his choices, he does not have free-will in his consequences. The killer had to face God's judgment. There was no way out of it—and he knew it!

For those who love God, His title of Judge brings comfort and peace! Perhaps the true mercy of the mark was on Cain's family through the reminder that God would take care of this horrific event, providing them rest both internally and externally.

In our day, legal trials can go on for months or years. Families of victims face many ups, downs and unknowns. They wait and hope that justice will be served. Their hearts wait for rest and settlement.

Not seemingly so with Adam and Eve. Adam and Eve did not have to wonder why Abel was missing. They didn't have to send out a search party. They did not have to question Cain or attempt to figure out if he was lying. They did not have to discover evidence or the body of their son. They did not have to wait for a conviction or punishment. They did not even have to come up with which level of punishment should be given.

I can almost hear Adam and Eve let out a long breath of relief which brought their heart rate back down to normal—or as normal as it could be while they mourned their losses. The all-knowing Judge would let them face their loss of Abel while He handled the case; while He handled Cain. What compassion our Judge demonstrated to these first parents!

Lastly, the mark **distinguished** him. It gave Cain a permanent mark of convicted murderer. It identified him as the one who had slain Abel. Years into the future, the mark would remind him of his past in a way that would plague him.

Sins that are dumped at the cross are removed from us as far as the East is from the West (Psalm 103:12). But those who choose to remain in their sins also remain burdened by them. They are enslaved and tortured by them. David wrote, "How blessed is he whose transgression is forgiven, whose sin is covered" (Psalm 32:1 NASB). He also wrote, "When I kept silent about my sin, my body wasted away through my groaning all day long" (Psalm 32:3 NASB). Jesus erases sins, but as long as those sins aren't surrendered at the cross, we remain affected by them.

Perhaps Cain had a lack of consideration for more than just his brother. He did not regard the truth, the future or the consequences.

Remember that the mark was a result of Cain's refusal to repent. I'm convinced that if Cain had confessed and surrendered to God out of a sincere heart, there would have been restoration and healing. Instead of the *punishment* which led to Cain's *complaint* which led to the *mark*, I think a confession from Cain would have led to God's *mercy* which would have led to Cain's *gratitude* for the mercy which would have resulted with a *new identity; a new mark.*

Cain did not want God's label. He did not want his identity transformed. He decided to remain in the identity he had made for himself. The killer could have surrendered to the Keeper and the Keeper would have put His mark of love, grace, healing and righteousness on him. This mark would have preserved Cain for far more than just the moment. It would have kept him for all of eternity!

Look how Jude described our Keeper: "Now unto him that is able to keep you from falling, and to present *you* faultless before the presence of his glory with exceeding joy, to the only wise God our Saviour, *be* glory and majesty, dominion and power, both now and ever. Amen" (Jude 24, 25). If Cain had confessed his crime and surrendered, God would have marked Cain as "faultless!"

Blood Cry

Just before the pronouncement of Cain's punishment,

the Lord said, "The voice of thy brother's blood crieth unto me from the ground" (Genesis 4:10b).

We already know that Abel's "answering of the fool" silenced Cain. Because Cain was not willing to surrender, he attempted to silence Abel. The only way that he could do that, or so he thought, was to physically shut up his mouth from speaking another word. He believed he could silence Abel through bloodshed.

Genesis 4:10b points out that Abel had not stopped talking just because he was dead. His blood still spoke (Hebrews 11:4). Cain's actions did not shut him up after all.

The question then becomes, "What did his blood say?" I believe Abel's blood spoke at least three things: **prophecy**, **faith** and **justice**.

The **prophecy** was to all the generations of people in history who would be born *after* Abel but *before* the birth, death and resurrection of Christ. The blood of Abel was a prophecy that pointed to the One who would fulfill the promise of atonement. It was the picture of the Seed that would give His life, shed His blood and rise again.

Secondly, Abel's blood spoke and continues to speak a **faith** message to Christians that will encourage them to completely trust God. His example through Scripture has been left as a spoken message that is needed generation after generation.

Cain could send Abel to the grave. He could dig a hole and cover his body with dirt. But He couldn't shut up the voice of Abel's example or the written Word of God. Killing Abel could not defeat God's work.

Even today, the killing of martyrs cannot silence God's people. It cannot cancel the spreading of Christianity. If anything, the murder of one martyr influences the rising up of many more voices!

Thirdly, the blood of Abel not only spoke but actually

cried out for **justice**. After the Lord said that Abel's blood cried to Him from the ground, He immediately acted with judgment toward Cain. There was no delay on his punishment. Abel seemingly cried out to God to vindicate him and bring due justice on his brother.

Listen to these words in Revelation:

> When the Lamb broke the fifth seal, I saw underneath the altar the souls of those who had been slain because of the word of God, and because of the testimony which they had maintained; and they cried out with a loud voice, saying, "How long, O Lord, holy and true, will You refrain from judging and avenging our blood on those who dwell on the earth?' And there was given to each of them a white robe; and they were told that they should rest for a little while longer, until *the number of* their fellow servants and their brethren who were to be killed even as they had been, would be completed also. (6:9-11 NASB)

Abel's blood cry was for God to vindicate him. The act of judgment toward Cain was a picture of the future judgment that will be placed on Satan and those who refuse to surrender to God.

Although Abel was the first martyr and his voice shrieked out that first blood cry, Psalm 116:15 says, "Precious in the sight of the LORD *is* the death of his saints." Even though Abel left this world tragically, I think all of heaven would eventually rejoice in receiving him.

Matthew 5:10 tells us, "Blessed *are* they which are persecuted for righteousness' sake: for theirs is the kingdom of heaven." This is Abel. His murder would be turned into a blessing; a joy; a completion.

The word *blood* in "the voice of thy brother's blood crieth unto me" (Genesis 4:10) is the Hebrew word, *dam.*[24] This word is *plural* in the original language of this passage—literally *bloods.* Some think that this plural form of the word is a reference to Abel's legacy. They think it speaks of the blood of those that did not have a chance to come from his line because he was murdered first. Another possibility is that it speaks to the blood of all those that would be martyred throughout history.

A third possible meaning of the plural word *blood* is that it speaks to Abel's *every drop of blood.* Many commentators agree that this word is used to show *quantity.* This means that there may have been a high level of violence to the crime. Cain may have struck Abel over and over until all of his blood was sprinkled from his lifeless body.

Another indicator that this is true is found in the New Testament, where the book of 1 John describes Cain as the one who *slew* his brother (3:12). The word *slew* refers to a slaughter or brutal laceration or disfiguration. Certainly a large *quantity* of blood would have resulted from this kind of killing.

Hebrews 12:24 speaks about blood in the context of Jesus and Abel. It says, "And to Jesus the mediator of the new covenant, and to the blood of sprinkling, that speaketh better things than *that* of Abel." This verse is likely paralleling two things that are alike: the sacrifice of Jesus and the sacrifice of Abel (whether it was his sheep or himself). Jesus and Abel were alike in many ways. They both likely sprinkled the same amount of blood. It was not necessarily that Jesus spilt *more* blood. The contrast was in the *effects* of those two bloods. Although both Jesus and Abel may have shed the same *quantity* of blood, they did not sprinkle the same *quality* of blood! Only Jesus' blood had resurrection power!

In many ways, Abel foreshadowed Jesus:

- Abel and Jesus both shed their blood because of their love for God and humankind.
- Abel and Jesus were both killed when someone else's power, pride and position were threatened.
- Abel and Jesus both died despite their innocence.
- Abel brought a lamb to sacrifice to God and Jesus was the lamb who laid down His life!
- Abel's blood spoke a prophecy of the One to come and Jesus' blood fulfilled the prophecy.
- Cain (physically) fled from the crime scene of the blood of Abel and the world (spiritually) fled from the crime scene of the blood of Christ.
- Abel's family likely ran to the crime scene of the blood of Abel and those who want Salvation run to the crime scene of the blood of Christ!

Though we can draw the parallelism between Abel and Christ, there is one major difference: The sheep's blood from Abel's sacrifice was only a *temporary covering*. Abel's blood only *covered the ground* and then sunk into it. Jesus' blood—that blood *covered our sins*! His blood covered my sins; your sins!

I am thankful for the blood of Abel which pointed many to Christ. I am a million times more thankful for the blood of Jesus that became the only way to the Father!

Jesus' blood crushes the confidence of eternal death! His resurrection awards us the security of eternal life. No other blood has power like His!

Before Jesus Christ came to earth, I think eternal death was doing a premature victory dance. Perhaps death was so confident that it was winning, it forgot to factor in the power of Jesus' blood. It had a false security in itself—one that would come crashing down with a major blow!

When the resurrection of Christ defeated death, it struck its ego! The high that it had been "living" on was flattened and squashed. How embarrassing for eternal death! And what a relief for those that death believed it had its steadfast grip on (1 Corinthians 15:55).

Yes—Jesus' blood speaks better things than the blood of Abel. His blood speaks better things than anyone because it speaks better things than eternal death! It speaks two wonderful words that we're not quite finished with. Let's reference the book of Jude yet again as we look to who Jude was writing to. He said, "to them that are sanctified by God the Father, and preserved in Jesus Christ, *and* called: Mercy unto you, and peace, and love, be multiplied" (vv.1-2).

First, Jesus' blood speaks *preservation*. It speaks eternal life. Once we have surrendered at the cross, we are set in the palm of His hand forever. No one; nothing can extract us from Him. Our identity is secure because His identity is established. We are eternally preserved in the One who proved that death could not defeat Him.

Just as Cain killed Abel, the soldiers pounded nails in Jesus' hands, pierced his side and laid him in a tomb. But Cain could not stop Abel from an eternity with God because no man could keep Jesus from rising again!

Second, Jesus' blood speaks the word, *faultless*. Jesus' blood was perfect (1 Peter 1:19). It was innocent. It was entirely pure. No other blood could have taken our place on the cross even if it wanted to. Only a blood that was faultless could in turn present us as faultless.

Oh, how we need the blood of Jesus! We need the cross...

On the Cross

At the final breaths of Jesus, He spoke seven statements from the cross. One of them came after a small conversation between the two thieves that hung on their own cross on either side of Jesus. Though these two thieves began their crucifixion by ridiculing Jesus, one of them decided to remain a "Cain" no longer.

Through the humble confession of his own sinful state and the verbalization of his belief in the innocent identity of Jesus, this man heard a beautiful promise from the Savior's lips, "today you shall be with Me in Paradise" (Luke 23:43b NASB).

Though the criminal on Jesus' other side heard His direct words and witnessed the confession of the other thief, he refused to surrender to the One who could save him for all of eternity. Though he was *physically* so close to Jesus, he was *spiritually* so far away!

Jesus died for both thieves. He loved both thieves. He loved Cain as much as He loved Abel. But the choice is left to us to either surrender and accept His love offer or slander and reject it. "To remain a 'Cain' or not?" That is the question!

Other last words that flowed from Jesus lips were, "It is finished!" (John 19:30b NASB). In other words, "It is completed." In those moments on the cross much was coming to a completion.

First, all of the work that Jesus had been sent to earth to do was now complete. His earthly ministry, perfection and obedience were accomplished.

In addition, all of the Old Testament foreshadowing and prophecies had been lived out through the life of Jesus. The literal picture of the two seeds from Genesis chapter three, that Cain and Abel represented, was coming to pass through the serpent bruising the *heel* of Jesus at His death on the cross but Jesus bruising Satan's *head* through His resurrection. The power over Satan and sin was being fulfilled.

Lastly, the transaction of all of our sins that was placed on Jesus was complete. The swap had taken place. The payment had been processed. Jesus had become a curse for us (Gal. 3:13). He was made to be sin for us (2 Corinthians 5:21). He did it all so that we could become the righteousness of God; so that we could be reconciled to God. He brought all of this to a completion so that we could be made complete!

Oh, how He loves us! His love is extensive—its depth is bottomless and its width is limitless. The love of God is flawless and relentless. Something so amazing is often so unattainable, yet God has made it so convenient and accessible.

The fact that God, while He existed perfectly and harmoniously without us, knew historically all that would take place and still went ahead and created us is beyond me. It speaks to one thing: how much we are worth to Him!

We were worth creating! We were worth being created in *His* image. After falling for the lies of the identity thief, we were worth rescuing. God did not consider us easy to let go of, replaceable or even despicable. We were worth chasing after and retrieving. A chase that was not pain-free.

The God of the universe who never needed to grow up from infancy, face and resist temptation, learn and gain knowledge, suffer from rejection and pain and experience the process of an agonizing death, did all of that for you and I. All while our back was against Him and we were active in sin, our Creator died for us. While we acted toward Jesus how Cain acted toward Abel, Alpha and Omega pursued us completely!

He did it because He loves us. He did it because we are

worth it. He did it because we *were* His creation from the beginning and He wants us to be His new creation *now*.

His resurrection power has brought you new life. Your worth is found there. Your new identity originates there. You are *complete* and secure in the One who made you, loves you and unsparingly gave His *every drop of blood* to redeem you!

There is a place where we can go to trade the sinful mark we acquired at birth with the mark of love we can attain for eternity! There is a place where we can be saved from an eternal separation from God and brought into a right standing with Him. There is a place where we can make a swap! *The cross.* We swap the first time for Salvation but we swap again and again for renewal as we live out our time on earth.

With Christ, we are no longer defined by our sins. With Him, we are no longer labeled "Guilty." We can surrender the old mark and receive a new and permanent one. Not only does God take off the bad, but He puts on the good. When we surrender the old, we are not left empty. God gives us something new. **Surrender the Old, Receive the New!**

Perhaps you are saved but it's been a long time since you've visited the cross. God is waiting for you to return there. Even after Salvation, the cross is a place we still need. Life abounds at the cross. We are changed at the cross! There is no better location for sinners to run to than the cross.

Nothing is better than the blood of Christ. If you've washed once, you know that. If you've stepped away for a time, I know you're missing it. If you've never washed, now is your time. Rare and expensive tangibles are costly and meant for the privileged. Oh, but the blood of Christ, which is the best of anything anyone could get, is so free and available to all.

Take the swap!

At the cross…
Swap your faults for His perfection
Swap your pain for His healing
Swap your sorrow for His joy
Swap your chaos for His peace
Swap your hate for His love
Swap your lies for His truth
Swap your sin for His grace
Swap your insecurity for His assurance
Swap your corruptible treasure for His everlasting treasure
Swap your emptiness for His completion
Swap your mark of death for His mark of life!

Chapter 9

Legacy

My Life, My Legacy.

And Cain went out from the presence of the LORD, and dwelt in the land of Nod, on the east of Eden. And Cain knew his wife; and she conceived, and bare Enoch: and he builded a city, and called the name of the city, after the name of his son, Enoch. And unto Enoch was born Irad: and Irad begat Mehujael: and Mehujael begat Methusael: and Methusael begat Lamech. And Lamech took unto him two wives: the name of the one *was* Adah, and the name of the other Zillah. And Adah bare Jabal: he was the father of such as dwell in tents, and *of such as have* cattle. And his brother's name *was* Jubal: he was the father of all such as handle the harp and organ. And Zillah, she also bare Tubalcain, an instructer of every artificer in brass and iron: and the sister of Tubalcain *was* Naamah. And Lamech said unto his wives, Adah and Zillah, Hear my voice; ye wives of Lamech,

> hearken unto my speech: for I have slain a man to my wounding, and a young man to my hurt. If Cain shall be avenged sevenfold, truly Lamech seventy and sevenfold. And Adam knew his wife again; and she bare a son, and called his name Seth: For God, *said she,* hath appointed me another seed instead of Abel, whom Cain slew. And to Seth, to him also there was born a son; and he called his name Enos: then began men to call upon the name of the LORD. (Genesis 4:16-26)

> A righteous man who walks in his integrity—
> How blessed are his sons after him. (Proverbs 20:7 NASB)

Building Nod

Each of us who continues on a family line will leave a legacy to the next generations. Who we *are* becomes how we *live* and how we *live* becomes an example to who *they* may *become.*

The family line of Cain not only knew his story but some carried on his wickedness of heart and action.

Cain's choices moved him away from the presence of his family and God. He settled on living in a land called Nod which was located East of Eden. This may have placed him even further from the perfect garden God had originally designed for man. Cain chose to *rest* in uncertainty. He chose to *settle* on identity crisis. He chose to build his life on the land of insecurity!

The Bible says in Genesis 4:17, "And Cain knew his wife; and she conceived, and bare Enoch: and he builded a city, and called the name of the city, after the name of his son, Enoch."

Because the Bible does not record the marriage of Cain at this point, he likely was already married before his move to Nod. It also does not seem logical that this woman would willingly marry and move away with a murderer if she was not married to him already—and quite possibly just as entangled in sin as he was. Whatever the status was of the relationship of Cain's wife and God, she suffered the effects of her husband's choices.

Many have asked the famous question, "Who was Cain's wife?" The answer is simply that he married his sister or niece. Marriage to a sibling or close relative was not yet forbidden by law—and genes had not yet been so affected by sin as to cause deformities. It is stated in Genesis 5 that Adam had other sons and daughters. We also find that in Genesis 3, Eve is called the "mother of all living." We can conclude that Cain married an offspring from his parents.

When Cain arrived in Nod, he built a city. I think the meaning behind this building is three-fold.

First, Cain was looking for a **purpose**. The favor of the ground yielding good crops for Cain had been taken away and therefore Cain sought to do something different with his hands. He needed something to do that would keep him motivated.

Second, I think the walls of the city reflected Cain's attempt at creating his own **provision** and **protection**. His removal from the presence of the Lord could not have made him comfortable or confident. Though his parents and other family members may have slept peacefully under God's care, Cain was motivated out of fear to build walls with his own hands as a defense against those who may still seek to kill him despite his mark.

Like Cain, many seek internally to put up their self-created walls of protection. When our relationship with God is suffering, it is because we have *moved* from His presence due to our sin. Living in sin has never made anyone secure. In fact, it can be quite frightening to live in a land away from God. 1 John tells us, "There is no fear in love" (4:18a NASB). Because Cain held onto his hate, fear could not be driven out of him. As a result of his sin, Cain attempted to build an infrastructure around his heart which no longer had God's protection. It was all he could do since he had chosen to remain outside of the Lords will.

Even as Christians, we often attempt to build these structures due to hurt, sin or disappointment. When these kinds of walls go up, it's because we are attempting to provide our own security and protect ourselves from further hurt.

Each wall that Cain put up had a name like anger, resentment, bitterness, stubbornness, jealousy, hurt, rejection, etc. Cain had been building around his heart for a while now. As he moved to Nod, his hands produced what was already deep within him.

Third, Cain built the city to carry on the **prosperity** of his line. Cain named the city after his son Enoch. Psalm 49 was written of those who place their trust in wealth. The Psalmist declared that no man can carry his riches into eternity, nor can he buy his or anyone else's ransom. He stated, "the fool and brutish person perish, and leave their wealth to others. Their inward thought *is, that* their houses *shall continue* forever, *and* their dwelling places to all generations; they call *their* lands after their own names" (Psalm 49:10b-11).

The point is not to say that nothing should be left to your children, but that your life should not be tied up in earthly materials. Your inner person should not dwell on a kingdom that will not last. Your name should not be left or spread to a world for the purpose of worldly fame. Your heart and mind should be on the kingdom of God and your name known by *Him*!

Certainly Cain had misplaced his trust and therefore he ended up in the land of Nod. He focused on his earthly palace as he sought to rebuild his false confidence. In hitting an all-time low through the punishment of God as well as essentially becoming the "world's most wanted," he did not crawl into a hole somewhere and hide out or disappear. Instead, he sought the construction of his own glory as well as the multiplication and glory of his own seed. The city of Enoch, by the line of Cain, flourished with inventions and developments which were likely marked and broadcast to the world with the highest level of pride as to who the inventor and developer was.

The prospering of the ungodly is a topic that has troubled many followers of God. Psalm 73 captures the psalmist's struggle with this issue. As he seeks the Lord in his situation, the Lord reveals that though the wicked may prosper on earth, their end will come and they will be consumed with terror in a single moment.

Verse 20 states, "As a dream when *one* awaketh; so, O Lord, when thou awakest, thou shalt despise their image." These wicked men who seemed to prosper were only living in a fantasy dream world. They would awaken to reality at the end of their life and face judgment.

This verse displayed that God would awake, or rather, rise up and despise the very image of the wicked like someone would dismiss a dream after waking. The wicked have no substantial identity to hold on to. Their *prosperity* will be short-lived!

In conclusion, Cain was still living up to the meaning

of his name in an earthly way. He was still producing and acquiring earthly treasures. He was also still living up to his character. He was all about himself. For a man who wanted a big house and city, he sure missed out on the biggest mansion and most beautiful city of all—heaven.

Cain had refused God's Kingdom. In a practical sense, what else would he do with the short time that he had left except build up his own earthly one?

Cain's Line

For an earthly time, Cain's wickedness carried on with success. Cain's son, Enoch, continued the line to Irad and from Irad to Mehujael, and from Mehujael to Methuseal, and from Methuseal to Lamech.

Lamech was the first person mentioned in the Bible to marry two wives; that is, he was the first mentioned polygamist. One wife was named Adah, and she had two sons named Jabal and Jubal.

Jabal was "the father of such as dwell in tents, and of such as have cattle" (v.20). Remember that they were living in the early stages of the world. Tents were a new invention and Jabal was probably able to design them due to resourcefulness and skilled handiwork. Since he cared for cattle, he likely developed tent living so as to have a home that could easily move to the places they drove the cattle.

His brother Jubal, on the other hand, was skilled with the harp and organ. Since he was called the father of these instruments, he was likely the designer, carpenter and developer of them. He must have had a natural-born ear for notes, tuning and pitch.

Have you ever met such a talented type of person and thought, "If only they would come to know the Lord and use those skills to serve God"? This is all I can think about as I look at the line of Cain!

Lamech's other wife was named Zillah and she had a son and a daughter. She first bore Tubalcain who was skilled with brass and iron. He was probably a type of early blacksmith. Tubalcain's sister was Naamah. Some believe her to be the wife of Noah, though nothing more is mentioned of her in the Scriptures.

On one particular day, Lamech said to both his wives, "Hear my voice; ye wives of Lamech, hearken unto my speech: For I have slain a man to my wounding, and a young man to my hurt. If Cain shall be avenged sevenfold, truly Lamech seventy and sevenfold" (Genesis 4:23b-24). This is nothing more than pride and stupidity talking. Typically, when someone is arrogant, they will brag about something they did. They will take it even further by bragging about the justification of *why* they were able to do it the *way* that they did—as if they have outsmarted God's laws against doing wrong.

When Lamech said that he should be avenged seventy and sevenfold because Cain was avenged sevenfold, he had surely picked up on the wrong message of his great-great-great-grandfather's story. He was making a mockery here by allowing license to sin and diminishing the seriousness of his crime.

The number *seven* appears as one of the most significant numbers in the Bible. The number *seven* often reflects the concept of completion.

For example, God created the world in six days and on the seventh day he rested from his completed work. In the well-known account of Joshua, his men encompassed Jericho seven times on the seventh day with the blowing of seven trumpets by seven priests. This resulted with a completion of victory. Other references to seven are found in the book of Revelation: among them, the seven churches, the seven angels, seven seals, seven trumpets and so on. The book of Revelation is the completion to the Bible that contains descriptions of the end times.

Other *sevens* in the Bible include God telling Elias, the prophet, that He had seven thousand men that had not bowed down to Baal (Romans 11:4). In Proverbs there are seven things that are an abomination to the Lord. There are also the seven "I AM" statements from Jesus in the book of John.

In Leviticus, Moses was spoken to by the Lord about a Sabbath for the land and people of Israel. Six years they would work the land and the seventh year they would rest. After seven Sabbaths (seven times seven, which is forty-nine years) they were to blow the trumpet of jubilee throughout all the land and hallow the fiftieth year. Clearly, their work was completed as they rested for a time and season.

In Genesis 4, there are two instances where the number seven is mentioned. First, Cain was going to be avenged *sevenfold*. But, what does the *sevenfold* part actually mean? When we look at the Lord's declaration that said Cain would be avenged *sevenfold* for whoever kills him, it can likely indicate that *complete* vengeance would be taken.

Cain had not received the worst level of punishment from God in the sense that God did not completely wipe him out. He did not strike him dead on the spot. Perhaps God allowed Cain to live because He had a purpose and plan that included Cain's line for a time. Perhaps Cain did not commit pre-meditated murder, but the person who would hunt down the location of Cain for the kill in another land would have pre-meditated that revenge. That person would've also gone against God's direct sign to not harm Cain. Maybe it's this person who would receive the fullness (*sevenfold*) of God's vengeance.

The second instance where the number seven is listed

in Genesis 4 concerns Lamech. He wanted to be avenged *seventy and sevenfold* for killing a young man that was trying to hurt him. Perhaps Lamech had killed more than once and therefore he wanted more vengeance. Or maybe he killed this man in (what he labeled as) "self-defense" and therefore thought that he should receive more vengeance than Cain who purposely killed innocent Abel.

Either way, Lamech seemingly attempted to reassure his wives that no harm would come to him for the murder he committed. In the Genesis narration, he speaks to them through poetry. Perhaps Lamech had a talent for song and poetry writing and yet used his gift to explain away his sins and declare how his life would play out. Lamech, like Cain, is just another example of how pride can take over our life.

In these verses, Lamech practically mocks God by taking matters into his own hands and announcing his own judgments. Perhaps, in the way that Cain was eager to whip out his anger and use it, Lamech was eager for an excuse to whip out his sword and use it—perhaps a sword made by his son, Tubalcain, who was skilled in iron!

Likely there was much more behind the murderous act committed by Lamech than he was claiming. This was not simply a justified self-defense case. Lamech was undoubtedly a wicked man who followed in the wicked line of Cain.

Impure motives and a twisting of God's judgments were surely a part of the whole picture. His declaration of how he should be avenged only points to his guilt. There is no evidence of humility here! Like Cain, there is no perceptible brotherly love.

Lamech wanted double vengeance, but the New Testament reveals *double sevens* in the spectrum of mercy. In Matthew 18:21, Peter asks Jesus how often he should forgive someone who had sinned against him. He questions, "seven times?" Jesus replied, "seventy times seven."

It wasn't a specific number that Jesus relayed, as if we should keep tabs. Rather, it was the opposite. We should forgive completely and without limits.

Perhaps by God's providence, another "Lamech" is mentioned in Genesis. This Lamech was a descendent of Seth (younger brother to Cain and Abel), the son of Methuselah and the father of Noah. He lived to be 777 years old. His death occurred just a few years before the flood. Multiple completions would have occurred around this time: the complete building of the ark and the preparations entailing it, the completion or ending of the pre-flood world, the complete covering of the world with water and the completion of the life of Lamech.

Perhaps, without superstition, the number *seven* should be looked at as a reminder of God's complete detail. His detail is so significant that we truly cannot understand the depth of it. Maybe all of this is a reminder that there is nothing beyond His knowledge—and that He is working, not only in the intricacy of the moment, but throughout all of time.

> **God's hands are cascading strategically, deliberately and brilliantly from creation to completion.**

Building a New Line

Though the line of Cain was quite instrumental in material developments, some were quite destructive in eternal matters. Cain's poor choices and identity issues were passed from one generation to the next. His life's story left behind an ungodly example. **My Life, My Legacy!**

If your family line has produced wickedness for

generations, know that you can be the one to disrupt that pattern. If you were born in the land of Nod and grew up under the influence of parents or relatives like Cain, you still have the choice to run the other way and escape—or for that matter, just surrender right where you are and ask God to carry you out!

Perhaps you grew up with no spiritual or godly influence in your family. Or perhaps you grew up with godly rules or rituals but no relationship with Jesus. If so, God can still do a work in you. No matter how you grew up or how old you currently are, you are not too far gone nor are you too late to enter God's family. He is *Abba*, meaning, *Daddy*. Take His hand.

My grandfather on my mother's side grew up as one of fifteen children. His home was filled with a level of religion and morals but he did not know Christ as his Savior. In 1956 my grandpa married the love of his life. God was after him because this woman, my grandmother, was a Christian. After a few years of my grandma taking my mother and aunt to church every week, my grandpa was finally saved in 1966.

He was baptized the next year. Not long later he helped build a new church building for Immanuel Baptist Church, here in Syracuse. My mom was of the first to be baptized in the new building.

After coming to know Christ as his savior, my grandpa's mission was to spread the good news. He witnessed to family and friends over the years, bringing some to their knees. In his old, retired age, he would visit and witness to complete strangers in the area hospitals.

To my brother and me, he was grampy-goopins. He was the one who would take us on fishing and duck pond adventures, make the best pancakes the morning after spending the night, and use us as an excuse for a McDonald's trip.

There were other memories, like watching his favorite show (Popeye) or combing his thick, white hair while he lay in his most comfy spot on the floor, or his worrying about us holding the railing down the fifty stairs from his home.

There's the fact that he worked construction by trade, including the grounds of the reconstruction of the Statue of Liberty in 1986 and that he served in the Army. He played guitar and harmonica by ear, he was the only one to call me by my real name (Jaclyn) and we even celebrated our birthdays together.

There's also the last day I spent with him: Valentine's Day of the year 2000. He went several places that day, including the local grocery store to get all kinds of candy and goodies for my brother and me. I saw him after school and all was good. I even dreamt about him later that night, but by the time I woke up, he had already gone to be with Jesus, his one true love! He was in the middle of writing me a letter when he must have fallen asleep and passed on due to a third heart attack.

Recently my mom located more letters from my grandfather that he had written sometime during the last two years of his life. Towards the end of one of those letters, he said this: "Jaclyn, your grandfather would pray that you would *continue* to look to the Lord as you do now, when you get older. Jaclyn, your mom and dad brought you up in a Christian home with lots of love."

Do you hear where the concern is? Do you hear what was important to him? It was the *continuance* of a godly family line.

The godly legacy had *started* with him, it continued to my mother, and my grandfather's letter was a reminder that it should *continue* with me too!

Seth's Line

Abel never had a chance to continue on a line himself, but God would grant mercy by giving Adam and Eve a specific child to "replace" him. Genesis 4:25b says that Eve "called his name Seth: For God, said she, hath appointed me another seed instead of Abel, whom Cain slew."

Adam and Eve lost their first two sons. Even here at the birth of Seth, Eve's heart did not forget that loss. Seth means "substituted."[25] God was not only merciful to Adam and Eve by "replacing" Abel with Seth, but He was merciful to all of us because of the line that proceeded after him.

The last verse of Genesis 4 says, "And to Seth, to him also there was born a son; and he called his name Enos: then began men to call upon the name of the Lord." Enos means "man, mortal."[26] Perhaps Seth named his son Enos because he had come to know that the life of man was short and weak compared to eternal, immortal and almighty God. In other words, the distinction of identities was recognized. Weak and temporal man needed strong and lasting God!

The phrase, "then began men to call upon the name of the Lord" (v.26) immediately follows the name Enos. This phrase has two possible meanings.

The first is that man was now calling *on* the Lord in a different way than before. Quite possibly the way that man communicated to God was different now that much sin had entered into the world. God seemed to directly speak to Adam, Eve, and even Cain, but at some point that changed. This is not because God changes but because man's sin marred the image of God's original design.

The verse states, "then began" as if something different started that had previously not occurred. Perhaps people began seeking God as a community of worshipers now that more people were on the earth.

The second possible interpretation is that men began to call themselves *by* the name of the Lord. In order to distinguish themselves from the line of Cain or those that did not belong to the Lord, they labeled or identified themselves as God's people.

In both cases, I believe that the line of Seth and other family members (excluding Cain and some living in Nod), took on the identity as followers of God. They may have done that both individually and corporately. Either way, we have men seeking God through the line and family of Seth.

Luke 3 denotes in further detail the exact line of Seth, laying out the line of Jesus through Joseph in a genealogy that goes all the way back to Seth and of course, Adam.

The last verse of Luke 3 reminds us (in case we had forgotten!) that Adam "was *the* son of God" (v.38). The lineage of the *son of God* led all the way to the *Son of God*! God had a plan from the beginning. He was working His way throughout history and each person in the line fulfilled the next step that eventually concluded with the Savior.

Can you see the clear difference between the line of Cain and the line of Seth? Cain sought to build an earthly city and a material inheritance to benefit his own pride. Seth sought to build a spiritual kingdom and an eternal legacy to benefit others hearts.

Jesus came through the line of Seth!

Continuing a Long Line

Mary Dumas, who is removed by seven generations from my father, had a heart for her family line. She was born in 1763 in Dutchess County, New York. Her husband Pierre was born in France in 1756.

Pierre was from Bergerac which is on the Dordogne River. In 1778, he boarded the 'Le Cezar' as a sailor in the French

Fleet bound for the West Indies. By day three of their voyage, officers announced a letter from the King which stated that France had joined the war siding with the "boys of Boston" and their ship would have to anchor in Delaware instead.

Due to storms at sea, the duration of the trip took them at least twice as long as expected. The British had moved on from Delaware by the time they arrived. The second plan was to barricade the harbor at New York. Instead, they made it to the Sandy Hook Harbor, just a couple miles from the New York Harbor, which shone forth America's oldest lighthouse first lit in 1764. There, the ships acted as a blockade just outside the harbor.

After their mission, they sailed the ships to Boston for repairs. For whatever unknown reason, Pierre chose to remain in America after landing there. He enlisted as a private for three years, serving in both Captain Treadwell's and Captain Wright's Company. In 1781, he re-enlisted and was sworn in at West Point. By the next year, he was chosen, under strict guidelines, to serve as a part-time guard for General George Washington who would become the first president of the United States a few years later.

By summer of 1786, Pierre and Mary were married. Five of their seven children were born where they resided in Dutchess County, NY. Pierre had become a carpenter after his service in the Army ended. Payment for his service had, in part, come in the form of land. In 1805, after trading and selling land on and off, Pierre and his family became the first settlers in Sterling, New York. A road marker with his name can still be located to the left of highway 104A Eastbound.

Mary did not endure an easy life, but she did fulfill one that was pleasing to the Lord. Settling in a new land with no one or nothing around her, all while raising seven children, must have produced many challenges. On the flip side, maybe it was kind of similar to the early days of the world that Adam and Eve faced. I'm sure they must have been inventive and creative.

Mary was also one of the first members to organize what would later officially become Hannibal Baptist Church. Worship and meetings were held in the homes of the members for several years. Missionaries would often visit and preach to the townspeople. The first church building was not established until 1827 in the village of Hannibal. That building still stands today as the Hannibal Community Center, which contains the Hannibal Free Library and the Hannibal Historical Society.

Mary was strong in the Lord and led the family toward Jesus. Throughout her life, Mary endured the loss of her son Ezra due to starvation, the loss of four grandchildren in a tragic and deadly fire, and the loss of her husband in 1825.

At the loss of her four grandchildren, ages nine, six, three and about nine months, Mary knelt before the Lord. In a poem that was written of the horrific fire, it was written of Mary that "She knew that God did for the best."[27]

Though the event was painful, it was also written that she "had laid up her *treasure* where it won't corrupt, which gives her strength and grace to bear her trouble, though it is severe."[28] Mary was known to be a woman of strong belief in God. A shorter poem that she wrote displayed her care for the eternity of the souls in her family line. This poem is inscribed on her tombstone:

My children dear, I pray draw near
and listen while I tell
Without free grace your dwelling place
will be a burning hell.

Mary and her family had much to *settle* in an unknown land, yet there was one thing that had been *settled* long before then—her heart. Colossians 1:23 says, "If ye continue in the faith grounded and settled and *be* not moved away from the hope of the gospel which ye have heard." Her *heart settlement* brought much care and concern about her family line.

Mary and Pierre bore seven children, including John Dumas. John married Nancy Church and they bore Nathan Dumas. Nathan married Sarah Abbott and they bore Elizabeth Dumas. Elizabeth married William Barrett and they bore Lizzie Beulah Barrett. Lizzie married Robert Lawyer and they bore my grandmother, Roberta Elizabeth Louise Lawyer (Betty). My grandmother married Edward Lloyd and they bore three sons, James, Robert and David, the eldest being my father. My father, James, married my mother, Karen Jandrew and they bore my brother, Jake and I.

My grandma (Betty) has testified of her knowledge of both her parents' and grandparents' relationship with the Lord. Certainly, I can testify to the fact that my grandma loves the Lord. She is known to me as a woman of prayer and I am thankful for her godly example. It is also a joy to report that my parents, my uncles listed in this family line and my brother are following the Lord as well. To see my family line written out, knowing so many of them have trusted in Jesus, encourages my heart to continue to leave a godly legacy myself!

Though Mary did not know what the future generations would hold, she did her part in our family line to leave a godly legacy. In a new and vacant land, Mary had no audience to act or look good for. Instead, she lived faithful to what the Lord called her to do with true godly character.

She left a legacy which would speak to many generations to come.

It was important to her that her children, her children's children, and all those after her, including myself, knew about God's grace and His offer to rescue us from eternal flames. Her passion for the Lord impacted one generation to the next. And I, for one, am beyond grateful.

Whatever blood you were born with biologically for your short time on earth, there is another blood of much more importance that will impact your eternity. The blood of Christ gives life and you can leave a legacy about the Source of the true blood that matters!

What part in history do you play that will point the future generations to the Savior?

> **Your godly effect on those to come may hinge on your present call to obedience.**

Chapter 10

I AM

Who God Is, Who I Am

> who do you say that I am?" (Matthew 16:15 NASB)

> I am Alpha and Omega," says the Lord God, "who is and who was and who is to come, the Almighty. (Revelation 1:8)

God has declared His identity throughout His Word. He has shown himself strong, faithful and loving from the beginning of time. He has not changed and He is calling you to trust Him.

As you read through the following list, know that there is no other God but Him. Know that there is no one else whose identity can be described like Him. Right here and right now, His voice is telling you who He is!

I am Alpha (Revelation 21:6)
I am Creator (Genesis 1:1)
I am Savior (1 John 4:14)
I am Father (Isaiah 64:8)

I am the Son of God (1 John 4:15)
I am the Spirit at work in you (Romans 8:26, 27)
I am King of kings and Lord of lords (1 Timothy 6:15)
I am Almighty God (Genesis 17:1)
I am love (1 John 4:8)
I am good (Psalm 107:1)
I am perfect (Hebrews 4:15)
I am all-knowing (omniscient) (Isaiah 40:13, 14)
I am present everywhere (omnipresent) (Psalm 139:7)
I am all-powerful (omnipotent) (Revelation 19:6)
I am the Word made flesh (John 1:14)
I am with you (Isaiah 41:10)
I am enough (2 Corinthians 12:9)
I am a strong tower (Proverbs 18:10)
I am a renewer of strength (Isaiah 40:31)
I am the Lord who heals (Exodus 15:26)
I am forgiver (1 John 1:9)
I am peace (Ephesians 2:14)
I am Father to the fatherless (Psalm 68:5)
I am righteous (Psalm 11:7)
I am Judge (Psalm 96:13)
I am the answerer to your call (Jeremiah 33:3)
I am the root and offspring of David (Revelation 22:16)
I am the bright and morning star (Revelation 22:16)
I am the one who searches the minds and hearts (Revelation 2:23)
I am the one that lives (Revelation 1:18)
I am searching for sincere hearts (2 Chronicles 16:9)
I am singing over you with joy (Zephaniah 3:17)
I am building a home for you (John 14:3)
I am Omega (Revelation 22:13)

How awesome is God in just this short list! And it could go on much longer! To read and study God's Word is to learn more about who He is—and knowing who He is, tells you who you are.

You are loved (John 3:16)
You are a child of God (Galatians 3:26)
You are His (Psalm 139)
You are not alone. He is with you. (Hebrews 13:5)
You are saved by grace (Ephesians 2:8)
You are a temple of the Holy Spirit (1 Corinthians 6:19)
You have His Spirit (Acts 2:38)
You are an heir of God and joint-heir with Christ (Romans 8:17)
You are set apart (Jeremiah 1:5)
You are dead to sin (Romans 6:2, 11)
You are the apple of His eye (Psalm 17:8)
You are safe (1 John 5:18)
You are free (John 8:36)
You were made for God's Glory (Isaiah 43:7)
You are a new creation (2 Corinthians 5:17)
You are more than a conqueror (Romans 8:37)
You are crucified with Christ (Galatians 2:20)
You are the salt of the earth (Matthew 5:13)
You are an adopted child of God (Ephesians 1:5)
You are an overcomer (Revelations 12:11)
You are a bearer of God's image (Genesis 1:27)
You are God's workmanship (Ephesians 2:10)
You are righteous (Romans 3:22)
You are complete (Colossians 2:10)

Many will want to tell you who you are or who you should be. If your heart has surrendered at the cross, then you bear the identity of the one and only voice that matters! You can have confidence in declaring who you are because God has declared who you are in Him!

Hold onto what God says is true about you. Live out who God says you are!

Since a deeper understanding of God's identity provides a deeper understanding of our *own* identity, let's discover more about who He is through the seven "I AM" statements from Jesus in the book of John.

I am the Bread of Life

In John 6, Jesus fed the five thousand from two fish and five loaves of bread. He later escaped the scene by going up to a mountain alone. That evening the disciples sailed toward Capernaum, but fear arose as they saw someone walking toward them on the water. Jesus put their minds at ease by *declaring His identity*. He said, "It is I; do not be afraid" (v.20 NASB).

The next day the (previously fed) people sought the location of Jesus. When they found Him, they questioned when He got to the other side of the sea. Jesus answered them, saying, "you seek Me, not because you saw signs, but because you ate of the loaves and were filled" (v.26 NASB). Jesus' miracles were proof that He came from God, yet the people sought Him to supply their earthly desires and needs.

The people wanted Jesus to show them a sign to believe. They referenced the manna that their fathers had eaten in the desert under the leadership of Moses (v.31). Jesus had fed them once, but Moses fed their fathers over and over with the manna from heaven. Jesus fed the five thousand, but Moses fed hundreds of thousands. Jesus declared that it wasn't Moses that gave them bread from heaven, but that God gives true bread from heaven, which gives life to the whole world.

When the people relayed their desire for the kind of bread that gives true life, Jesus said, "I am the bread of life; he who comes to Me will not hunger, and he who believes in Me will never thirst" (v.35 NASB). The Jews *murmured* and *complained* at His statement and they questioned Him some more.

Jesus stated that their forefathers ate manna but still eventually died—because that bread was a temporary provision. Jesus said, "the bread also which I will give for the life of the world is My flesh" (v.51 NASB).

He was, of course, speaking all of this in a spiritual sense—as to say that only He can satisfy the cravings of our soul. We were built *by Him* with an inner longing *for Him* that nothing else can complete. He is the bread that offers eternal life.

As we consume the bread of life, the satisfaction to our soul is fulfilled. Until that happens, we speak *murmurings* of *discontentment* and *disgruntlement* like the Jews did. As we allow *His* identity to complete *ours*, it is out of a satisfied soul that our lips produce beauty and praise.

Even as Christians, we can become swiftly diagnosed with a contagious disease called *negativity*. We move from complaining about one thing, to complaining about everything, to seeking out things to complain about. We have forgotten that Jesus is our fulfillment that brings contentment to our soul. Our souls crave spiritual food when they aren't filled up with Him.

Psalm 63:5 says, "My soul shall be satisfied as with marrow and fatness; and my mouth shall praise thee with joyful lips."

Instead of murmuring about and questioning Him, start *believing* and *praising* Him.

Jesus is the bread that gives life to your soul. **Feed on Him!**

I am the Light of the World

John 8:12 says, "Then Jesus again spoke to them, saying, 'I am the Light of the world; he who follows Me will not walk in the darkness, but will have the Light of life'" (NASB). Jesus declared that He is light. If we follow Him, *we* will have the light.

After Jesus spoke the words, "I am the light," the Pharisees (religious leaders) reacted by saying that Jesus was giving witness of Himself and what He was saying was not true. I love Jesus' response: "Even if I testify about Myself, My testimony is true, for I know where I came from and where I am going; but you do not know where I come from or where I am going" (John 8:14 NASB).

Do you hear what He is saying? He can declare His own identity because of what He knows about the past and the future. He knows where He came from: He came from God. He knows where He is going: He is going to heaven for all of eternity.

The Pharisees lived by the law that "the testimony of two men is true" (Deuteronomy 17:6). Jesus explained that in this case, He was one witness and His Father was the other. The Pharisees questioned where His Father was and Jesus replied that if the Pharisees truly knew *Him*, then they would also know the Father.

The Pharisees couldn't speak of their own identity with confidence and truth like Jesus did when He said, "I am the light." They were lost as to who they really were because they did not know the Father. Since they did not know the Father, they couldn't know the One who was light. If they had no light, they couldn't see who they were, where they came from or where they were going. They were stumbling in darkness.

John (in 1 John 2:9-11) reveals to us the depth of why a

person may lack light. He makes the connection between love and light with equation-type statements:

Loving your brother = Light = No occasion for stumbling

Hating your brother = Darkness = Not knowing where you are going

This "equation" shows that the Pharisees had the same problem as Cain: they had no love. The Pharisees had followed all but the two greatest commandments. Love was missing, and because of that, light was missing too!

1 John 4:7-8 puts it this way: "Beloved, let us love one another, for love is from God; and everyone who loves is born of God and knows God. The one who does not love does not know God, for God is love" (NASB).

God is the ultimate light source because He is the absolute love source!

For those of us who do love Jesus, I wonder how our light looks to a world in darkness. What if the world had no physical light? No sun. No moon. No stars. No electricity. No flashlights. No candles. What if everything was pitch black, with the only light source being followers of Christ? How bright would your light be? Would your neighbors seek you out as a light source? Would they run to your house because you were the only light on the block? Would it make them want the same light you have?

Like people running to a brightly lit home in this scenario, people will run to a love-lit home in the real world. As a person in darkness will not care to run to a house that has a dim or flickering light, they will not care to run to a house that offers minimal or spastic love either.

As we begin to love deeper and wider, our light will shine brighter and fuller!

Jesus is the light of the world. **See by Him!**

I am the Good Shepherd - I am the Door

John 9 recounts Jesus' healing of a blind man. Jesus spit on the ground, made some mud, placed it on the blind man's eyes and told him to wash in the pool of Siloam. The blind man followed His instruction and came back from the pool seeing, though Jesus had already left the area.

Since this man was known to have been blind from birth, his healing instigated all kinds of interrogation from witnesses and later the Pharisees. Initially, this man had no knowledge of Jesus' true identity; he was only able to testify that a "man called Jesus" had healed him. However, as the now-seeing man repeats his testimony to the unbelieving Pharisees, he becomes increasingly aware of who Jesus is, finally saying, "if this man were not of God, he could do nothing" (v.33). At this the Pharisees threw the man out, understanding that he was identifying Jesus as the Christ.

When Jesus heard that the man had been cast out, he approached him again and asked, "Dost thou believe on the Son of God?" (v.35). Because the man had previously said that Jesus was a man "*of* God," Jesus was leaning into him to draw out a deeper confession: the confession that Jesus *was* God Himself.

The man responded, "Who is he, Lord, that I might believe on him?" (v.36). Remember, he had heard Jesus' voice but had not yet seen him. Surely he recognized that voice because, although he did not yet believe Jesus *was* God, he believed that this man who had healed him *knew* God and had the answer as to where his faith should be placed.

I think he was looking for an "I AM" statement that would confirm what he was already beginning to believe. Jesus supplied it with the words, "You have both seen Him, and He is the one who is talking with you" (v.37 NASB). The man then worshipped Him, saying, "Lord, I believe" (v.38).

The next chapter of John brings us to the identity words of Jesus, "I am the door of the sheep" (10:7 NASB) and "I am the good shepherd" (10:11 NASB). In this passage, Jesus explains that His sheep know His voice and they follow Him. He knows them by name, and goes ahead of them and leads them.

Though we do not know the name of the man who was once blind, Jesus did. He used His voice and spoke to him. He went ahead of him and directed him to receive his sight and the man followed His instruction.

I love how Jesus did His work with the mud and then left the ultimate choice to the man to either obey Him by going to the pool and washing or not. It looks a lot like the picture of the cross. Jesus did His work and now the choice is up to us to either follow Him or not; to wash in the fountain of His blood or not.

Even after the man received his sight, he knew the voice that had once opened his eyes and now he sought Him to open his heart. Once the identity of Jesus was confirmed to him, he immediately believed.

How can we know the voice of the good Shepherd? How can we know Him and follow Him?

The answer is in the last few verses of John 9, in which Jesus says, "For judgment I am come into this world, that they which see not might see; and that they which see might be made blind" (v.39). The Pharisees hear this and question if they too are blind, and Jesus replies, "If you were blind, you would have no sin; but since you say, 'We see,' your sin remains" (v.41 NASB).

Jesus was saying that it all comes back to humility. Like Cain, the Pharisees thought they could see. They thought they had all the answers on their own and that they had no sin to confess. The sin that both Cain and the Pharisees demonstrated was pride, which was founded on their own ability and wisdom.

Those that represent the blind (in Jesus' reply to the Pharisees) are like Abel. They admit they have no ability to see without Jesus. They hear His voice, follow that voice to the pool, see Him and eventually know Him because they have emptied out *self* and are filled with his *I AM*.

The voice the Pharisees heard was their own repetitions of their so-called goodness—as if they had to convince themselves of it. They thought that they could complete their identity by following the letter of the law through Moses. Like Cain, they were blind to the truth that they really were *not* following the law because they did *not* have love for their neighbor. Rather, they used the law as an excuse to execute their hate.

There are days when my son JJ has a tough time seeing past what he has already set his mind on. Usually it's over (what seems to us as) silly things. For instance, one day he wanted blue paper to put stickers on. We were out of blue paper. No matter how I said it, or how many *times* I said it, somehow he could not seem to hear me telling him that we were out of blue paper.

Instead, he kept demanding and repeating over and over, "Blue paper! Blue paper! We do have blue paper!" As his inner battle continued and turned into tears, I asked the Lord to show me what to do since this type of problem was an ongoing issue with him. In that moment, the Lord helped me to understand that before he could listen to *my* voice, his own voice needed to be silenced.

I firmly but genuinely looked at my boy and said, "Stop. Don't say *blue paper* anymore."

His reply? "Okay, Mama. I'm sorry."

What had seemed like a battle that would never end, ended in a single moment when his own repetitious voice was silenced through sincerity and authority.

After his voice, heart and mind were calm, I was able to explain to him that we really were out of blue paper and that it was okay to choose another color. He listened to my voice and believed what I was telling him.

The same is true for us, who are like sheep. The voice of Jesus (our Shepherd) is heard and learned when the other voices, including self, are eliminated. Humility is the eliminator.

The voice that needs to be muted may not be a spoken voice, but the one that resounds in our heart or mind. We need to silence our inner demands, our repetitions and our declarations of our own wisdom and desires. Sometimes we need to sit silent before the Lord with a surrendered heart (Psalm 46:10).

Romans 10:17 says, "So then faith *cometh* by hearing, and hearing by the word of God." Other times, we need to let God's word pour into us. His voice can be found there. Once we hear that voice and respond through Salvation, we will hear that voice over and over again through His "I AM's." It's a voice worth following because the leader is good!

This shepherd is so good that He laid down His life for His sheep. And as Jesus said, as recorded by John, "This is my commandment, that ye love one another, as I have loved you. Greater love hath no man than this, that a man lay down his life for his friends" (John 15:13).

Like a shepherd who lies in the doorway, guarding any

access to his sheep in the pen, Jesus laid down His life for us. Nothing and no one can separate us from Him. **He is the Door.** The wolf cannot sneak by and steal a sheep. Once in His fold, always in His fold.

As Jesus leads us out of the pen, we listen for and follow His voice. He gives us peace, restoration and comfort regardless of whether it's on the highest mountaintop, through the darkest valley, by the calmest waters or in the midst of a furious storm. He walks us through each day no matter what it brings. Whether he calms the storm (Psalm 107:29) or not, His voice is directly behind our ear, whispering, "This is the way, walk ye in it" (Isaiah 30:21).

Despite how loud the storms of life become, they cannot surpass the voice of our Shepherd. It's not that His voice rages louder than the noise of the storm, but that His voice is always closer than the storm! Nothing can come between Him and us.

Jesus is the Good Shepherd and the Door. **Listen for Him! Follow Him! Enter in through Him!**

I am the Resurrection and the Life

John 11 recounts the death of Lazarus, the friend of Jesus and brother of Martha and Mary. As Jesus arrives in Lazarus' hometown, he is met by Martha, who professes that her brother would not have died had Jesus only been with them in Judea. She knows that Jesus could have prevented her brother's death.

In response, Jesus tells Martha, "Your brother will rise again" (v.23 NASB). At first, Martha assumes Jesus is referring to Lazarus' resurrection at the last day, not his recent life on earth.

Jesus says, "I am the resurrection and the life; he who believes in Me will live even if he dies, and everyone who lives and believes in Me will never die. Do you believe this?" (vv.25-26 NASB).

Martha believed Jesus even though Lazarus had been dead for four days. As they arrived at Lazarus' tomb, Jesus had the people roll the stone away and He called forth Lazarus. Lazarus came back from the dead at the command of Jesus.

The belief of Martha, Mary and probably others allowed them to see the glory of God (John 11:40). They were witnesses to a piece of God's identity; the piece that contains life and power over death itself.

Are we not witnesses to that part of God's identity as well? The physical picture of Lazarus portrays the spiritual transformation of all those who come to know Christ as Savior. Jesus brings us back from the dead. Our heart and soul are revived through faith in Jesus.

The account of Lazarus ends with two verses which show the two different effects on those that witnessed his resurrection. Verse 45 tells us that many believed in Jesus and verse 46 tells us that some left the scene and went to the Pharisees.

When Jesus changes our hearts (not just when we receive Him as Savior, but any time throughout our walk with Him) or demonstrates His power in our lives, others will witness that radical phenomenon. Some will marvel at God's work and be compelled to change and others will walk away wanting no part of it.

Certainly Cain witnessed the spiritual resurrection of Abel, yet chose to remain spiritually dead. I don't think it's too much to propose that Abel's spiritual resurrection may have impacted some of his other siblings differently.

We must not be fearful of the possible outcome of a person's heart when the miracles of God in our lives are made known to them. We must not sit back and live a mediocre life with caution that we might offend someone or be mocked by them. For it is by witnessing the miracle in us that some will choose Christ! Let others see the resurrection of your heart in your daily life.

Jesus is life. **Live in Him!**

I am the Way, the Truth and the Life

This "I AM" statement from Jesus followed a question from Thomas who said, "Lord, we do not know where You are going. How can we know the way?" (John 14:5 NASB). Thomas was unsure how they could know the way if they didn't know the place He was headed. Thomas was likely wanting to know the name of the town or city to which Jesus was going so they could journey the path to get there. His mind seemed to be on earthly matters rather than spiritual.

First, Jesus answered his question about how to know the way. He said, "I am the way, the truth, and the life" (v.6). Next, Jesus answered Thomas' lack of understanding about where He was headed. He said, "no one comes to the Father but through Me" (v.6 NASB). Jesus was telling Thomas that He was going to His Father.

Jesus proclaimed on several occasions that He and the Father are *one*. In John 14:11, He says, "Believe me that I *am* in the Father, and the Father in me." He also tells his disciples that the Father would give them the Spirit of truth which would be their Comforter (v.26). If they know Jesus, they will know the Father; and it's that Father who would give them the Spirit. In this passage, Jesus clarified the union between the three (Father, Son, Spirit) in order to help his disciples see the *way*.

"I am the way, the truth, and the life" (v.6) was spoken by Jesus as a direct declaration of His identity. He is not just *a* way. He is the *only* way. He is not just someone *speaking* truth. He *is* truth itself. He is not just offering us a *good* life nor is He himself *just* a good person. He is the designer of physical life, the giver of spiritual life and *is* life everlasting.

The destination is the Father. The way is Jesus. Many have attempted various roads to get to God. Cain attempted to win God's favor with his own works and labor. Later, in Genesis 11, others tried to build a tower to reach heaven. Throughout time, countless peoples and cultures have attempted other religious or ceremonial acts to secure their afterlife with God. There is an obvious gap between us and God which man desires to bridge.

However, all efforts to gain Salvation without the Savior are failing! There is no other route by which you can get to God. Just as angels, rulers, powers and anything else in all of creation cannot separate you from the love of God once you belong to Him, those same things cannot bring you to God either.

Jesus is the way, the truth and the life! **Trust Him!**

I am the True Vine

In John 15, Jesus says that He is the true vine and we are the branches. He continues, "As the branch cannot bear fruit of itself, except it abide in the vine; no more can ye, except ye abide in me" (John 15:4). The word "abide" means to *remain* or *stay*. Jesus was telling us that we need to stay connected to Him in order to bear fruit.

What does it mean to remain in Him? Remaining in Him is to admit that He is the vine and we are the branch. To leave Him is to say that we are our own vine and that we do not need Him. Saying that we don't need Jesus is declaring that we can earn our own way to God, or at least our own way in life. "I don't need the vine," one may say.

Instead of saying "I don't need God," others say, "I don't want God." They say this when they accuse God of having too many rules to follow. What they really mean is that they don't want anyone telling them what to do. "I want out of the vine!" they say. But God's law is not oppressive to those who know the victory and freedom that is found by remaining in the vine.

There is a third party that combines the two: "I *am* the vine." This person actually likes the idea of the vine—only they want to be it. In an attempt to look good, sound good and even feel good to themselves and others, they have sought to display that they are connected to God (or at least that they can act godly or good), except they have placed themselves as the vine and Jesus as one of many branches that they control.

This is undoubtedly what Cain did. He made it look like he had a connection with God, yet he did not make Him the supreme authority in his life. He tried to switch the identities of the Vine and the branch. Spiritual fruit did not flow from him simply because he was not the vine, nor was he connected to the vine. He did not abide.

God is the "keeper of the vineyard" (and Jesus is the Vine) because He exists entirely on His own. He does not need us. He is life itself. We are the branches because we only exist, both spiritually and physically, because of God. We need Him. We are dead without Him. We carry no life powers on our own, therefore we cannot bear fruit on our own.

2 Timothy 2:13 says, "If we are faithless, He remains faithful, for He cannot deny Himself" (NASB). God cannot change. He will not conform for us. He is who He is. If we choose not to believe, God will not make Himself into a branch for us. He is the Vine. We are the branches. And the only way to be connected to Him is to abide in Him. The proof that we are abiding is in the fruit.

The way to abide in Him is to keep the identities of the Vine and the branch as they truly are. We cannot just attempt, on our own, to be good like Jesus was. We cannot say, "I will just try to walk, talk and live like Jesus." The fruit of being like Jesus comes when we say, "You are the Vine and I am the branch." More fruit is produced when the "keeper of the vineyard" (the Father) prunes us.

Jesus is faithful to remain the Vine. Remain the branch. Do not attempt to go off on your own. You will not survive because you are not the Vine. Be who you were designed to be. Be the branch!

> **Saying and admitting, "I am the branch" not only brings us back to humility but it puts our identity and purpose back into perspective!**

Later in John, Jesus goes on to say that God is glorified when we bear much fruit. He is glorified when we remain as the branch because that is how the fruit grows. According to Jesus, if we abide in Him, our joy will be complete. True joy flows from living out our true identity as a branch.

For Valentine's Day last year, my Mothers of Preschoolers (MOPS) group gave each mom a red paper heart on which to write a message for our husbands. Since the heart wasn't too big, the message had to be short. At first thought, the words, "Be Mine" came to mind. But… am I the only one who thinks it sounds silly to say that to someone who is already yours?

The next thought that crossed my mind was that, those who are saved are already God's. He doesn't need to say, "Be Mine." However, He is saying the exact thing that I wrote on the Valentine heart to my husband: "Remain Mine!"

Tell him now in a short prayer that you are thankful for His faithfulness as the Vine. Then tell Him that you want to be faithful in remaining as His branch.

Jesus is the Vine. **Abide, remain and stay in Him!**

I AM THAT I AM

God is the ultimate I AM. Our true identity can be found in Him because He is our Creator and because we were made in His image. How amazing is it that He is who He is!

What does it mean for God to say that He is "I AM?" Exodus 3 depicts the account of God directing Moses to go before Pharaoh and bring His children out of the bondage of Egypt. God had heard the cries of the Israelites and had witnessed their oppression. God appeared before Moses in a burning bush and relayed the message that He would send him to Pharaoh.

Moses was wondering who he was that he would be able to accomplish what God was telling him. Perhaps his insecurities were creeping up on him. He was also unsure how he should answer the people of Israel when they asked who the name of the person was that sent him to them. God instructed Moses to tell the people "I AM THAT I AM" had sent him.

I love how Moses was changed because God declared who He was. Moses' identity became secure with God's "I AM." This is how God changes us all. The more we hear about, learn about, experience and yield to God's identity, the more we can live out our true identity completely.

If we "fast-forward" to the end of the Bible, Revelation 1:4 says, "John to the seven churches which are in Asia: Grace be unto you, and peace, from him which is, and which was, and which is to come; and from the seven Spirits which are before his throne." This phrasing of "which is and which was and which is to come" is more than three separate phrases strung together; it's a single title that reflects "I AM THAT I AM" in the Exodus passage.

When Moses voiced concerns, God said He was going to be with him in his present situation. He said, "Certainly I will be with thee" (Exodus 3:12). This is the One "Who Is."

God continued to instruct Moses to tell the people that "The LORD God of your fathers, the God of Abraham, the God of Isaac, and the God of Jacob, hath sent me unto you" (v.15). This is the One "Who Was."

After that, verse 17 says, "And I have said, I will bring you up out of the affliction of Egypt unto the land of the Canaanites, and the Hittites, and the Amorites, and the Perizzites, and the Hivites, and the Jebusites, unto a land flowing with milk and honey." This is the One "Who Is To Come."

Though God expands into time much further than this Exodus passage relays, God was giving His people a reminder how He would help them in their present moment, that He was the same God of their fathers and that He would lead them to a land of promise.

Who is the "I AM?" He is the One **Who IS** and **WAS** and **IS TO COME**.

"I AM" is the all-encompassing identity of God; everything that makes Him who He is (combined from all duration of time). It's His complete character that resonates how awesome, mighty and eternal He is. There is no one higher. There is no one who stretches into time deeper. There is no other God but Him. He is it. He is all. Nothing exists *beyond* Him and all things were created *by* Him. Your search ends with Him here and now.

He is reminding you that He is with you in this present moment. He has not overlooked your oppression. He is here leading and directing you to victory. **HE IS.**

He is reminding you that He is Alpha, Creator and Redeemer. He was there before time began and nothing exists outside of His own hand. He made you. He loves you. He died for you. He is alive for you. He wants you. **HE WAS**.

He is reminding you that He is Omega. He will defeat the evil one. He has a land and kingdom of promise for you for all of eternity. He has a home that is overflowing with His goodness and He invites you there. **HE IS TO COME**.

It is no wonder that Billy Graham was able to say on national television in his My Hope America message, "I know where I've come from, I know why I'm here, I know where I'm going."[29] Such security in his identity only comes from one thing: knowing the One Who Is, Who Was and Who Is To Come!

Our identity becomes complete with the "I AM!"

After knowing the declarations of the "I AM's" of Jesus, there is only one thing left to consider. He is asking you, "who do you say that I am?" (Matthew 16:15 NASB).

Answering this question answers another question…

Who are you? What's at the core of your identity? What you believe about God will answer what you believe about yourself. The truth of who God is will tell you the truth about who you are!

The Core

As we look at the following diagram of God's identity, we see "I AM THAT I AM" at His core—the title of God's all-encompassing identity. The seven "I AM" statements from Jesus flow from that core. This is a clear picture of who God is (though there are many more "I AM's" that also stem out from God's core).

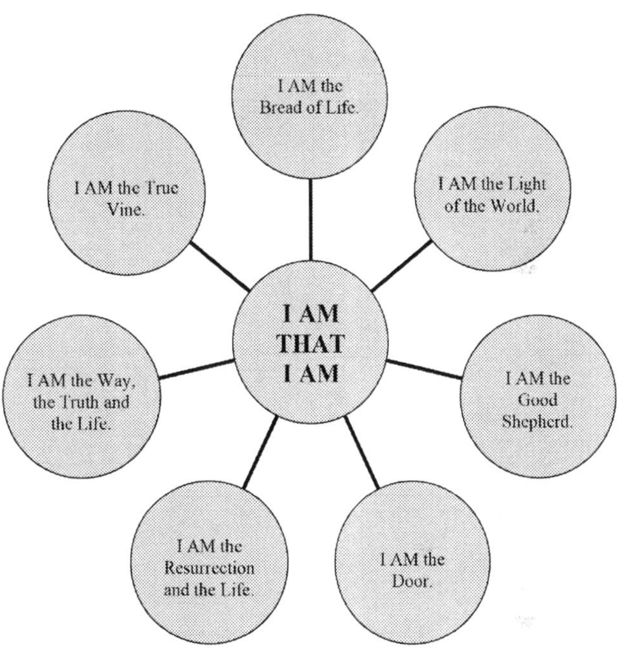

As we believe in and surrender to God, we receive our own "I am" from each of His "I AM's." We are able to confirm who we are based on who He is. God's identity tells me about my identity! **Who God Is, Who I Am!** Because "I AM THAT I AM" is at the core of His identity, the core of our identity becomes "I am His."

God's "I AM the resurrection and the life" gives us the truth of "I am back from the dead. I am revived. I am victorious." His "I AM the bread of life" becomes our "I am fulfilled and satisfied in my soul."

His, "I AM the way, the truth and the life" becomes our "I am on the *right* path to eternal life. I am who God says I am." His "I AM the good shepherd" becomes our "I am a sheep well cared for and spiritually led." Because He is the door, we are secure. Because He is light, we carry His light. He is the Vine and we are a fruit-bearing branch.

We receive our identity from His identity. When we believe and surrender *completely,* we live out who God has declared we are in Him. We become a living example of the true "us!" We experience all the internal benefits that He has for us. This diagram is what we look like in Him.

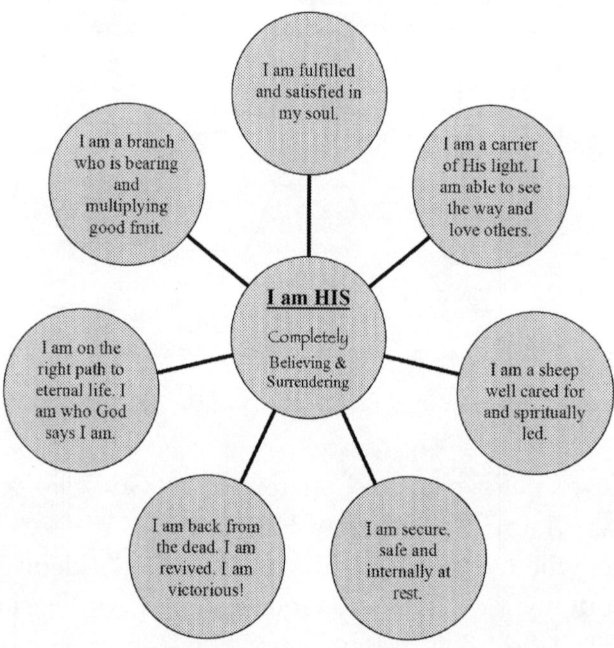

There is one more diagram. This is our how our lives look when we are partially doubting or resisting. We face certain effects when we aren't completely believing and surrendering.

Nothing can change the true identity we have in Christ. We are His forever. But sometimes we doubt a part of who God says He is and in turn, we doubt who He says we are. If we aren't *believing* a part of God's identity and therefore are doubting a part of our own identity, we begin to live out a lie. We live out what is against God's declaration of the truth. Here's how it looks:

We are His but... we doubt that we are fully revived when we doubt that God is the Resurrection and the Life. Instead of believing in God's identity, we become trapped in some sin that is weighing us down. We are His but... instead of fully believing that the "Bread of Life" is our fulfilment, we become a bit empty inside.

Ever find yourself compromising truth or wandering without direction? Do insecurities rise within you or fear overtake you? Do you wonder why you've lost your love or compassion for others? Are you tripping down life's path? Have you forgotten your purpose? Are you unsure who you really are? Are you tired of toiling with no spiritual fruit to show for it? If so, it's because you're living in doubt of what God says is true or you're resisting surrender to it.

This diagram reveals how our lives are affected without *completely* believing; without *completely* surrendering.

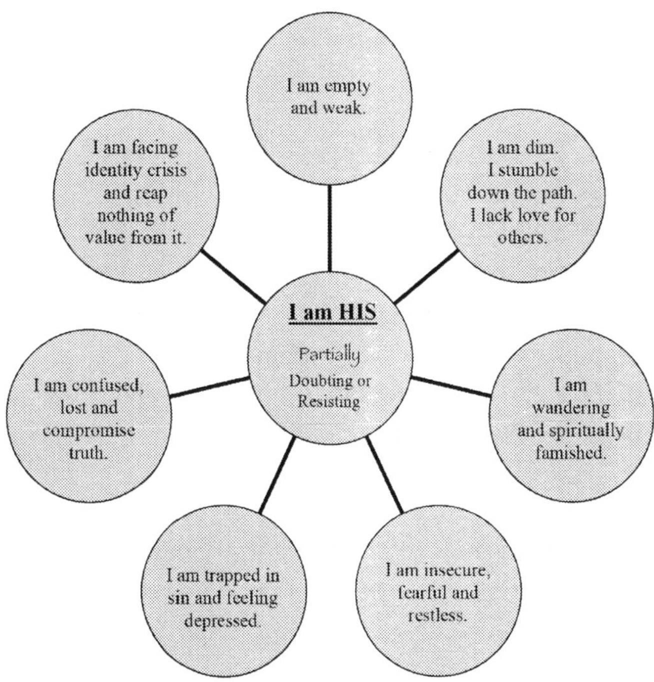

Look at the effects in your life when you doubt or resist in this third diagram. Get honest and determine which of these you are struggling to overcome. Next, match your struggle to the truth of God's "I AM" in diagram 1. Match it again to the "I am" He has given you in diagram 2. Finally, write out those two truths and think over them daily. Pray about them. Ask God to open your eyes, heart and mind to these truths when you are tempted to live out the lies in diagram 3. Tell God that you believe His "I AM" and surrender whatever you are resisting that is hindering you from living out your true "I am."

Certainly there are more "I AM's" of God and more "I am's" of us than these diagrams cover. We can take any identity issue that we are facing and apply the model of these diagrams. If you are feeling unloved, consider God's truth of "I am love" and live in the truth of "I am loved by Him." If you're feeling like a total mess, consider that God has said, "I am the Potter" and live the truth "I am a new creation." If you're living in past guilt, consider God's "I am forgiver" and live out the truth of "I am forgiven. I am clean." If you are living in sin, consider God's "I am defeater of sin and death" and live out the truth of "I have the righteousness of Christ. I am victorious in Him!" Take the identity issues in your life and replace them with God's truth. Then, ask God to help you live in the light of it!

God has declared His identity and He has declared your identity in Him. By faith, you can live out what God says is true! In doing so, you will reap all of His internal benefits!

The more fully we believe in who God is and surrender to Him, the more completely we can live out who He says we are!

Chapter 11

Knit Together

God's Glory, God's Grace

> And he said unto me, My grace is sufficient for thee: for my strength is made perfect in weakness. Most gladly therefore will I rather glory in my infirmities, that the power of Christ may rest upon me. (2 Corinthians 12:9)

> As for Mephibosheth, said the king, he shall eat at my table, as one of the king's sons. (2 Samuel 9:11b)

Grace

What is grace?

Grace is receiving the unearned favor of God. It's God giving us a benefit that our current identity or behavior does not warrant. Romans 3:24 says that we have been "justified freely by his grace through the redemption that is in Christ Jesus."

How do we get grace?

Grace is not something that we can buy or handle. It is not something that we can take and twist with our hands. If we think we have control over God's grace, we have been sadly fooled by a false image of it. Grace is so much bigger than us. It surrounds and envelops us. 2 Corinthians 12:9 says that God's grace is sufficient for us, and then concludes, "that the power of Christ may rest upon me." Grace is like a tabernacle. If we want grace, it is freely waiting for us. Just walk into it. Just surrender under its covering.

What is the effect of grace?

Though grace treats us gently in our frail state, grace is powerful because it changes us. The effect of grace is renewal. Paul says in 1 Corinthians, "But by the grace of God I am what I am" (15:10a NASB). Grace transforms our identity! It changes us.

> **God's grace is not handed to us so that we can abuse Him with it. God's grace tabernacles over us so that we can be renewed under it! His grace tabernacle has no entrance fee!**

Glory

What is glory?

The word "glory" in Hebrew is *kabod*—meaning *abundance*.[30] It has the idea of heaviness or weight. It's the weight of who God is. It's the beauty of His character and attributes. It's the vastness of His holiness. When we consider the abundance of all that God is, it's His identity.

In earthly terms, the glory of a bird is its wings and

the glory of a daffodil is its petals. It's the uniqueness of something. And what isn't unique about God? He is immortal, eternal, all-powerful, all-knowing, holy, just, creator, love, merciful, the beginning and the end and much more.

How do we declare glory?

Isaiah 43:7 tells us that we were created for God's glory. We were created to give and declare weight to who God is.

As we become renewed through the grace and mercy of Christ, we are now called to worship God and declare His glory through our life. Paul implores us in Romans 12:1b to "present your bodies a living and holy sacrifice, acceptable to God, which is your spiritual service of worship" (NASB).

In the same way that Abel surrendered a whole lamb to God, we are called to surrender the full sacrifice of our self! As Abel's lamb was pure, we are to live a holy life through the power of Jesus Christ. We have full access to victory!

We are called to be a freshly-showered, fully-breathing, heart-beating sacrifice for God! How else would we declare His glory but through every part of our being? Our life should tell the story of His glory! This is pleasing and acceptable to Him.

What is the effect of declaring His glory?

Romans 1:22-23 says, "Professing themselves to be wise, they became fools and changed the glory of the uncorruptible God into an image made like to corruptible man, and to birds, and fourfooted beasts, and creeping things."

An exchange is occurring here. It's the worst kind of swap anyone could make; trading the glory of the immortal God for images of all kinds. It's giving weight to something other than God. It's worshiping the *created* instead of the *Creator.*

It is no wonder that many are lost without any purpose or meaning in life. When we exchange the glory of God, we are exchanging what we are designed to do. We are exchanging who we are meant to be. We are exchanging our entire purpose!

Declaring the glory of God fulfills in us the meaning of who we are!

> **By declaring the glory of God, our hearts reap the benefit of being settled, fulfilled and complete!**

Where Grace and Glory are Knit Together

In the early nineteen hundreds, Helen H. Lemmel wrote a simple, yet astounding chorus that I sing to my boy each night.

> Turn your eyes upon Jesus,
> Look full in His wonderful face,
> And the things of earth will grow strangely dim,
> In the light of His glory and grace.[31]

There is a two-fold thing going on here—glory and grace. When we sin, it's often because we have forgotten God's glory, which diminishes His power and magnificence—or we adopt a false image of His grace by thinking that we can continue in our sin.

It is by remaining under grace that we are transformed into our true image of declaring God's glory! Grace and glory go hand in hand. They are "best pals." **God's Glory, God's Grace!**

The account of a king, his best friend and his best friend's son (in the book of 2 Samuel) shows us a clear picture of **glory** and **grace**. There are five main characters in this story, and each one is a **type** (symbol) of a "character" in a larger picture, as follows:

- King David becomes a **type** of God
- Jonathan becomes a type of Jesus
- Mephibosheth (son of Jonathan) represents all humankind (including Cain and Abel)
- The nurse represents Adam and Eve
- The Philistine army and Ziba represent the enemy and Satan

We will see how this literal story represents our own spiritual story.

First, we must set the stage. Saul was the king of Israel, and his son Jonathan was naturally in line to inherit the throne. However, Samuel (the prophet) had anointed David (a shepherd boy) to become the next king of Israel.

Sometime after David killed Goliath, a bond and friendship formed between David and Jonathan. 1 Samuel 18:1 tells us that "the soul of Jonathan was knit with the soul of David, and Jonathan loved him as his own soul." We are also told that the two friends made a covenant together (v.3) and that "Jonathan stripped himself of the robe that was upon him, and gave it to David, and his garments, even to his sword, and to his bow, and to his girdle" (v.4).

As the years passed, King Saul spiritually declined. Jealousy caused Saul to pursue David and to seek to kill him. However, Jonathan's heart was loyal to David and they made yet another covenant together that extended into the future. "The LORD be between you and thee, and between my seed and thy seed forever" (1 Samuel 20:42).

After seeking the counsel of a witch, Saul fought the Philistines at the battle of Gilboa and died there. His son Jonathan died at the same battle. Upon hearing of Jonathan's death, David declared, "I am distressed for thee, my brother Jonathan: very pleasant hast thou been unto me: thy love to me was wonderful" (2 Samuel 1:26).

As news spread of the death of Saul, Jonathan, and others, fear of the Philistines seemed to strike the nurse who was at the kingdom caring for Jonathan's five-year-old son, Mephibosheth. 2 Samuel 4:4b says, "and his nurse took him up and fled. And it happened that in her hurry to flee, he fell and became lame. And his name was Mephibosheth" (NASB).

The nurse was the "keeper" of Mephibosheth. She was supposed to take care of him, preserve him. Though her intentions to flee the enemy appear to be logical on the surface, she was also fleeing their home and the kingdom. Fear and a hurried state brought chaos and crisis to the scene, which resulted in a fall. This fall affected the son of Jonathan; Mephibosheth became crippled, unable to use his legs, because of his nurse's choice.

After these events, the nurse took Mephibosheth to live with Makir of Lo-debar. It cannot be entirely coincidental that the name of this place means "pastureless."[32] It's a place that is *barren*. Lo-debar was not only the place where Mephibosheth ended up physically, but it was also the place where he ended up mentally, emotionally and likely spiritually. He lived in a place that drained everything out of him.

Not only did this place lack a pasture, but I think it lacked communication. I think *words* were *barren*. There was likely no spoken dialogue between Mephibosheth and those at the kingdom during his years in Lo-debar.

As the years passed, the lineage of Saul grew weaker and David and his men grew stronger, until David finally became king over all Israel. When the battles ceased and life had finally quieted down for him, David asked the question that appears in 2 Samuel 9:1 "Is there yet anyone left of the house of Saul, that I may show him kindness for Jonathan's sake?" (NASB).

David had such a kinship and bond with Jonathan that he wanted to honor their friendship by showing kindness to someone in Jonathan's line. He did not forget his covenant with Jonathan, the one that included his descendants.

In order to find Jonathan's relatives, a man named Ziba, who was once a servant of Saul, was summoned to David and questioned. David's inquiry about Saul and Jonathan's line was many years after those two had died and David had become king. Mephibosheth was no longer a boy but an adult. Mephibosheth had kept his distance from David and the kingdom for a long time. Even though he had a connection to the kingdom through his father and grandfather, he had no ability to get to there. Though the kingdom was once his home and the place where he truly belonged, Mephibosheth had identity issues that kept him in a far off land.

Ziba answered David's inquiry. He said, "There is still a son of Jonathan who is crippled in both feet" (9:3b NASB). Ziba made sure he described Mephibosheth by his weakness! Based on the revealing character of Ziba in later passages (2 Samuel 16:1-4 and 19:24-30), it seems possible that Ziba may have been a degrading voice to Mephibosheth. Perhaps he had spoken the lies of Satan that diminished his value. He may have wanted the benefits of what David had to offer for himself and thought he could deter David from giving them to Mephibosheth if he belittled him.

David was unaffected by the mention of Mephibosheth's physical state and "fetched" him from Lo-Debar. Perhaps he used the information about his crippled state to figure out the best way to get him to the kingdom. Maybe David used an animal or servant to carry Mephibosheth due to his disability.

As Mephibosheth arrived and appeared before David, he bowed his head, showing reverence and humility. David called Mephibosheth by name and Mephibosheth declared that he was David's servant. David showed him kindness and joy, and restored to him the land of Saul and gave him a place to eat bread with him at his table forever.

Mephibosheth then portrayed the depth of his crushed identity by saying, "What is your servant, that you should regard a dead dog like me?" (9:8 NASB).

Mephibosheth was broken and lame. Not only did he describe himself as dead, but he equated himself as a dead animal. He practically labeled himself roadkill that no one cared about! You see, kings and their sons were warriors, fighters, heroes. They weren't lame. Mephibosheth believed that his current state disqualified him from having a connection to the king.

Over the years, Mephibosheth must have felt worthless and unwanted. Perhaps he had lost all sense of purpose in life. Maybe loneliness crept in as it may have been difficult or at the least challenging to go anywhere. Maybe he was ashamed and embarrassed by his lifeless legs. Perhaps his unfulfilled desire to have what everyone else had depressed him to the point of blocking people out of his life. Maybe he even became bitter with thoughts that blamed the fall, the enemy, the nurse and others for the curse that he faced.

Despair, depression and an utter darkness may have almost choked the life out of him.

Does this story have a familiar taste to it? David is a picture of God the Father, and Jonathan a picture of God the son. As David and Jonathan were "knit together," so are God the Father and Jesus Christ. The covenant they had was a redemptive one. The "pact" was that Jesus would come to earth to rescue the seed of Adam, and God the Father would raise Him from the dead as well as give the gift of the Holy Spirit to those who would trust in Him. This covenant between God and Jesus existed from the beginning of time, but it was sealed with blood at the death of Jesus.

The Father in all of His glory sent Jesus to demonstrate His amazing grace. Where are grace and glory knit together? In the identity of God! The abundance of God provided unearned favor. The covenant of grace and glory was fulfilled at the death and resurrection of Jesus. The grace of God and the glory of God are forever woven together!

The picture of Jonathan giving his most precious gifts to David is as Jesus who handed over his robe to God, left His Father's throne above, took on flesh, was born in a manger, became a servant and suffered a cruel death for our sake. Jesus gave it all up because of the covenant He had with His Father.

The nurse is a picture of Adam and Eve and the Philistines are a picture of Satan. Adam and Eve were called to "be fruitful and multiply." They were called to preservation and life. They were called to be "keepers" of God's creation and their offspring. When the enemy attacked them, they did not do as the book of James now tells us to do. "Submit therefore to God. Resist the devil and he will flee from you" (4:7 NASB). Neither Adam and Eve nor the nurse had the enemy running from them. Instead, our first parents fell for the enemy's schemes and the nurse caused the fall of Mephibosheth by fleeing their home.

The "fall" in the Garden of Eden affected all of humankind. Like Mephibosheth, a crippled state became the identity of every human ever born. Cain, Abel, and every offspring from the first parents lost the ability to be born and to exist in innocence!

Our departure from the original and beautiful state in which God created us has caused us to live in a place like Lo-debar. There is nothing of value to harvest when we are at a distance from God. There is nothing to gain outside of communication with Him.

It is when we are at a distance from God and out of communication with Him that Satan tricks us into believing that our King does not want us; that we are of no value to Him. As we believe Satan's lies and sulk in our shame, we begin to treat others in the same way. We devalue others by convincing ourselves that they too are not worth loving on, sacrificing for or reaching out to. We treat others in the light of what we believe about ourselves.

Like (a possible) Ziba to David, perhaps Satan even attempted to tell God that there was no reason to send Jesus to rescue such worthless "dead dog" sinners like us. If he did, it was a major fail!

Grace ran hard for us! As King David in all of his glory showed kindness because of Jonathan's sake, our most glorious God showed grace because of Jesus' sake. Like Jonathan, the death of Jesus Christ made it possible for us to receive restoration of our identity and our true home.

The grace of the King of kings carried us in our crippled and sinful state. Grace sought *us* out. We were not perfect before receiving grace. Grace located us in our dark, barren and Lo-Debar-like condition.

> **Grace has the power to move us from a land that is barren to a kingdom of benefits.**
>
> **Grace transforms us from the person that we've been to the person we were meant to be all along!**

Just as something tragic had happened to Mephibosheth, tragic things occur in our own life. We sometimes allow our crippled state to consume us and we sulk in our pain as we wonder, "why did this happen to me?" When things go wrong, we often want someone to blame. Perhaps Mephibosheth blamed the enemy or his nurse. We may blame Satan, our parents or others around us.

Perhaps though, Mephibosheth blamed the king. Ultimately and underneath it all, we blame our King. We blame God through our *refusal to believe* and our *refusal to surrender.*

Refusal to Believe

When we blame God for the curses that we face, we are often refusing to **believe** that God is good (and therefore we assume He must have caused this evil) or that God prevails over evil (and therefore He has no power to do anything about the evil).

When faced with tough circumstances, it can be easy to dismiss the fact that *God is good.* This is a simple truth about the identity of God, and yet we are quick to trade it for the Devil's lies which say that God is mean or that He is holding something back from us.

There are so many foundational principles of God's

identity that go all the way back to the book of Genesis and *God being good* is one of them. At the end of each day of creation God declared that all He had made was *good.* The creativity that He spoke, formed and breathed was good because it came from the divine goodness of its Creator.

In contrast to what Adam and Eve desired and tasted in their direct disobedience to God, Psalm 34:8 says, "O taste and see that the LORD is good; How blessed is the man who takes refuge in Him!" (NASB).

Believe that God's identity is good. His desire is for you to have the full benefits of His goodness! Don't trade it for a worldly gain. Don't swap it for a taste of lies.

When bad things happen, we sometimes refuse to believe that *God prevails over evil.* We fail to believe in His power.

On the surface, we know that bad things happen because Satan is evil and man has free-will to choose that evil. The deeper truth comes into play when we believe that the *glory* of God prevails over evil.

There's a line that I love from an old hymn that says, "That though the wrong seems oft so strong, God is the Ruler yet."[33] It all comes back to the beginning! We can live out our present faith in God through the worst of evils because we trust in the One who is Omega (ruler). He is Omega because He is Alpha and no one and nothing can change that!

Evil cannot prevail over God's glory! Like Cain, it can take its best stab for the moment, but it will not win in the overall picture.

Remember what God said about wicked Pharaoh, "For the scripture says to Pharaoh, FOR THIS VERY PURPOSE I RAISED YOU UP, TO DEMONSTRATE MY POWER IN YOU, AND THAT MY NAME MIGHT BE PROCLAIMED THROUGHOUT THE WHOLE EARTH" (Romans 9:17 NASB).

God can fulfill His purpose regardless of evil. Even when evil appears to be defeating God, His glory reigns! If our whole purpose is to live for His glory, then no bad thing that happens to any God-seeking person can prevail over our true purpose!

> **Evil cannot prevail over God's glory + My purpose is to live for His glory = Evil cannot prevail over my purpose!**

When the evil of this world reaches for you, it cannot ruin your purpose because it cannot surpass God's sovereignty. I wonder if our own bitterness towards the bad circumstances in our life is just a result of our own refusal to live for God's glory and believe in His power. Have we claimed the "right" to act poorly just because someone else treated us wrongly? Have we blamed the evil of others for ruining our purpose?

> **The most evil efforts of man cannot prevail over our purpose because they cannot surpass the sovereignty of God!**

Not long ago when my little JJ was learning to write the alphabet, he became quite frustrated. He cried buckets of tears and was unable to continue writing because the "K" was all wrong. After encouraging him to skip to the next letter, telling him it was "okay" because he was just learning, saying that he could try it again and everything else I could think of, he still sat there crying, unable to move on.

At some point I realized what he was really upset about. It wasn't just because he had made a mistake, but that his mistake made the page look bad. All of a sudden, something popped into my head. "Why don't we turn that mistake into a heart!" I said. He responded happily and was able to continue on with the rest of the alphabet after covering over that "K" with a beautiful red-penciled heart.

Bad marks on our life are just like this. We think they are ruining the picture of our life and God must be powerless to do anything about it. We'd rather sulk in our pain than believe in the God who has a plan to cover it with the beautiful mark of His love.

If we allow the curses in our life to consume us, we stop declaring glory to God. If we stop declaring glory to God, we lose our purpose. If we lose our purpose, we lose the benefits of joy and fulfillment.

1 Peter 5:10 provides comfort for those who are facing trials and struggles. "After you have suffered for a little while, the God of all grace, who called you to His eternal glory in Christ, will Himself perfect, confirm, strengthen and establish you" (NASB).

Look at what God does!

Perfect = He makes us complete!
Confirm = He props us up so we can stand!
Strengthen = He makes us strong so that we can walk!
Establish = He grounds and settles us on a firm foundation!

Romans 8:18 tells us, "For I reckon that the sufferings of this present time *are* not worthy to be *compared* with the glory which shall be revealed in us."

When we hold the present wrongs or evils in our life up to the weight of what eternity will bring, there is no comparison. The evil is like a small speck on the page that has been long buried by God's artistic redesign. His glory covers the page with its beauty and worth!

Will you trust Him with the pages of your life? Will you let Him write your story?

Believe that God's identity is all-powerful! Evil cannot take over the pages of your life. God is far mightier than whatever evil circumstances you face.

Believe in God. *Believe* that He is good and that He prevails over evil!

Refusal to Surrender

When we blame God for the evil that we face, we are not only refusing to believe God but we are refusing to **surrender** to God the effects of the curse (and therefore we make the effects an idol).

We can give glory to all kinds of *positive* images other than God, such as our family, car, house, career, beautiful appearances, etc. But just as we can give glory to positive images, we can give weight to *negative images*. Idolizing the positive images is often just a cover-up to make ourselves feel better or look better than the negative images that we suppress. Some of our deepest problems stem from giving weight to the effects of the curse.

Not only are we born with a sin nature and a depleted spiritual state, but sin and the acquired curse brought much pain and suffering into this world. We suffer, not just spiritually, but physically, mentally and emotionally. Examples of our suffering can include: health problems, learning disabilities, weight control issues, heart sorrows and many other things that effect our image. We even struggle with insecurities about how all these weaknesses look to others!

When faced with the effects of the curse, we often say things like, "I'm bound by this weakness," "I can't," "I will never do anything good," "God, why did you make me this way?," "It's not fair," "I am so stupid!" or "I hate myself."

These words may be secretly spoken in your mind as you look in the mirror or hit the pillow at night—or they may be spoken out loud as you sulk in them and even implore those around you to join in your misery. Either way, underneath it all is pride, shame, bitterness, anger, jealousy and refusal to surrender.

Sound a bit like Cain? Underneath the outward attitudes of pride and strength are the inward cries of insecurity and weakness. I think Cain's pride in production and strength in labor was a cover-up *for* or distraction *from* the weaknesses and identity issues he had as a result of the curse.

Like Mephibosheth for so many years, perhaps it's our shame that has kept us from returning to our Kings' presence. Perhaps it's our weaknesses, insecurities and inabilities that we often refuse to surrender. The effects of the curse have become an idol that we serve and are consumed with. I wonder though, what if our weaknesses are just an opportunity to see God's power at work? Isn't God bigger than our inabilities? What if God is just asking us to believe and surrender completely so that He can demonstrate His strength in us?

After all, isn't that what Salvation is all about? We first admit that we have a weakness and inability to save ourselves. We lack resurrection power. Through our confession, belief and surrender, God graciously demonstrates His power over our weakness! It is by this process that God gets the glory because we cannot take credit for what we could not do in the first place. As God gets the glory, we fulfill our purpose!

How do we go from having a weakness to fulfilling our purpose? How do we go from lacking a relationship with God to gaining an eternity with Him? How is it that we were once weak and now we are strong? We were once guilty and now we are innocent? We once had no ability to withstand temptation and now we have the power of Christ working within us to overcome the world, the flesh and the devil? We once worshiped a physical hindrance, but now God is using it for good? We once idolized a disability, but now we are living out God's plan in the midst of it? We once were barren and now we are filled with God's grace?

2 Chronicles 16:9a sums up the answer and all the lessons of Genesis 4:

> **For the eyes of the LORD move to and fro throughout the earth that He may strongly support those whose heart is completely His.** (NASB)

God is looking. He is looking to uplift those who admit they need supporting; those who admit they have a weakness. He is in search of those who have a sincere heart. He is not looking for a display of our strengths. The offering that God regards is the *frail heart* that says to Him, "Completely."

This was the heart of Abel. He was a frail and weak man who had a strong and mighty God. He experienced the faithful hand of God uplifting him in his weakest moment. He witnessed a display of God's strength through his own feebleness!

God is looking throughout the earth for more "Abel's." He is looking for a heart that resounds, "I am completely Yours!" Will He find that in you?

Do you believe that God can use your physical inabilities for His glory? Do you trust that God can take your spiritual weakness and give you victory? Are you willing to stop using your weaknesses as a blanket of comfort? Are you willing to surrender them so that you can fulfill the person God is calling you to be? Will you let go of whatever effect of the curse that has become your idol?

> **False pride and strength can be torn down in the light of God's glory and insecurity and weakness can be covered over in the light of His grace!**

Believe. Surrender. Completely.

Two of a Kind... Or are They?

Mephibosheth and Cain may seem to have opposite motives, but perhaps they have more in common than we might think. For instance:

- Mephibosheth believed the lie that he was no good because of his broken legs.
- Cain believed the lie that he was so good because he could produce and acquire.

- Mephibosheth thought, "Since I can't produce and acquire, I have lost my value, worth and acceptance of the king."
- Cain likely thought, "Because I'm so good at producing and acquiring, I will gain my value, worth and acceptance from God."

- When the king called Mephibosheth to his home, Mephibosheth wondered why the king would bother with such a worthless dead dog as he was. He may have thought, "I can offer you nothing. I am nothing."

- When God rejected Cain's offering, Cain may have thought, "How can you say I'm not good enough? I am amazing at what I do!"

- Mephibosheth had the idol of weakness and shame. He was bitter because of the loss of his legs.
- Cain had the idol of his strength and pride. The fear of losing his title and image kept him producing. He became angry when his self-made identity wasn't accepted.

Mephibosheth and Cain had the same core issue. Perhaps if God were to write letters to Mephibosheth and Cain, it might look something like this:

> Dear Mephibosheth,
>
> You're not worthless because you CAN'T produce. There's nothing so bad about you that My **grace** can't cover! Your worth is found in Me! Believe and surrender.
>
> With all My love,
> The King of all kings
>
> Dear Cain,
>
> You're not worthy because you CAN produce! There's nothing so good about you that can match My **glory**. Your worth is found in Me! Believe and surrender.
>
> With all My love,
> Alpha and Omega

Mephibosheth and Cain both placed their worth in something other than God. They believed that their value was connected to their ability to produce and acquire. They wanted acceptance but believed they had to earn it. How many times and ways do we do the same thing?

We become depressed, bitter, miserable, angry and distant from God over our weaknesses, inabilities, sin, losses and negative circumstances. Why would we not believe in the God of all grace who can cover over a multitude of imperfections?

We also become prideful, self-focused, haughty and temporarily gratified from our accomplishments, good looks, abilities, self-righteousness and positive circumstances. Why would we not surrender to the God of all glory who can secure our identity with His abundance?

Both Cain and Mephibosheth had an idol that they allowed to declare their worth. But idol worship is in direct contrast with what we already know about God's beginning. God will win in the end because He is Alpha and Creator. Idols cannot prevail because they are created by those who were created.

Idols are not self-existing. They don't appear out of nowhere. Hear the words of Habakkuk 2:18: "What profit is the idol when its maker has carved it, or an image, a teacher of falsehood? For its maker trusts in his own handiwork when he fashions speechless idols" (NASB). In other words, why would you worship what your own hands have formed? How could you let something that doesn't talk, declare your worth? The creator has more power than the creation!

Strengths and weaknesses exist, good and bad circumstances exist, wealth and poverty exist, talents and inabilities exist—but they don't exist as an *idol* until *we* form them into one!

Amazingly, the name Mephibosheth means, "dispeller of shame."[34] By sitting at the table of David, Mephibosheth's legs were situated under the table where he could no longer visually see his weakness. His shame disappeared because he no longer gave *attention* to his legs but fully enjoyed the food and communion offered at the table. Isaiah 30:22 says, "And you will defile your graven images overlaid with silver, and your molten images plated with gold. You will scatter them as an impure thing, *and* say to them, "Be gone!" (NASB). The king's table made shame dissipate. It said, "Be gone!"

The name "Mephibosheth" can also be broken down into the two words, 'pa'ah' and 'bosheth.' 'Pa'ah' means "to cleave in pieces"[35] or as some have described, "to break into pieces". 'Bosheth' means "shame."[36] Mephibosheth literally destroyed shame! He became an "Image breaker." It was as though his weakness had become an idol that needed to be shattered. The worship of that idol was sin and sin produced shame.

Essentially he was able to destroy this image and idol because of the love, grace and kindness of a king. He was able to break down the haunting whispers of Satan that told him that he was worth no more than a dead dog. The image of shame was shattered as his worth and place of belonging were declared!

"You belong here," David may have said.

David not only said that Mephibosheth would eat at his table, but after Mephibosheth revealed his crushed spirit, David said he would eat there as one of his *sons* (9:11). Beyond land and food, Mephibosheth was offered a new identity. It was the identity of being the son of the king. Healing was upon him. His image, purpose and place of belonging had been established forever.

Perhaps David publicized, "I present my son—Prince

Mephibosheth!" And perhaps Mephibosheth humbly bowed his head before the king, yet again!

When you let go of the idol you created, you are able to worship the God who created you!

Like king David to Mephibosheth, God is offering you the benefit of His table! Not only that, but He is offering you the outstretched arms of Jesus that will carry you there. The King of all kings has promised you an eternal home and inheritance. He has declared you as His son; His daughter.

He says, "You belong here. Child, you are Mine!"

Just believe and surrender. Let the goodness of the King wash away all of your identity issues! Fall into His arms that provide both the *power* to destroy the idol and the *comfort* to cradle you in your frailty.

Stop blaming God for the curses. Stop taking credit for your abilities. Instead, *believe* that God is good and powerful. *Surrender* whatever positive or negative idol you hold on to!

We often blame God for the curses in our life, but through our unbelief and lack of surrender, we're the ones running from all of His benefits!

We often steal credit for what we produce and acquire, but through our unbelief and lack of surrender, we're the ones missing out on all of His abundance!

Stop running. Don't miss out. Quit living in the depressing and degrading land of Lo-debar. Quit living on the highland of yourself.

The God of all **glory** and **grace** is offering to carry you in your crippled state and bring you to the table of His benefits!

After all, the same God who cursed the world with thorns in the garden is the same God whose head was pierced with those thorns on the cross! The King of all kings took the curse upon Himself for you!

Chapter 12

From Earth to Eternity

My Life, My Death, My Gain

> For to me, to live is Christ and to die is gain. (Philippians 1:21 NASB)

> One *thing* have I desired of the LORD, that will I seek after; that I may dwell in the house of the LORD all the days of my life, to behold the beauty of the LORD, and to inquire in his temple. (Psalm 27:4)

A Shepherd's Summary

After Abel's blood cried out from the ground at his death, I believe Abel himself spoke one more thing. It's the same thing he had likely spoken most of his life in the future tense, except now he was able to say it in the past tense. What was once, "It's going to be worth it" was now, "That was worth it."

All the pain, suffering, challenges and struggles that Abel faced in life were well worth remaining faithful. God was worth it. Abel must have faced trials in his job as the first shepherd. He must have faced the same tough days that we often face, like being tired, sore or sick. He certainly faced the struggles of resisting sin and temptation as well as the heart cries of confession for whatever sins he did commit. We can say with confidence that he had to deal with an opposing, dysfunctional relationship with his brother (and possibly others). He must have received flack about his prophetic actions that called others to repentance. He most definitely dealt with heartbreak from observing his brother's defiance against God. And there is no question that he faced pain as the first martyr.

Despite all of that, I believe Abel spoke the words, "That was worth it. God, You were worth it all!"

I do not believe that Abel would enter eternity and ask God why He didn't stop his brother from killing him. He wouldn't appear before God and get upset that He took him from earth all too soon. He wouldn't question who God was or why it happened the way it did. He wouldn't try to convince God that He should let him go back to earth and complete some bucket list.

Rather, we are the ones who do that. We do that at the death of a loved one when we don't understand. We do that when we try to reason with God why it should have turned out differently. We do that when we forget that this world is not our home. We do that when we don't *trust* God. We do that when our *surrender* is missing.

Not Abel, though. There was no looking back for him. There was nothing more desirable on earth and there was nothing about God that he didn't trust. In the presence of Almighty God, Abel would be made complete—and in that moment, he would kneel at the feet of Jesus and likely say, "Worthy is the Lamb!"

Abel's specific mission on earth was complete by

pointing to the grace of the coming Savior. He fulfilled the overall purpose of his identity, which was to declare the glory of God. I'm sure the following words would be said of him: "Well done, *thou* good and faithful servant!" (Matthew 25:23). Abel completed well!

Abel truly lived out the second half of Matthew 10:39 which says, "He who has found his life will lose it, and he who has lost his life for My sake will find it" (NASB).

Abel inherited far more than the earthly firstborn inheritance that Cain clung to and demanded. Cain was physically in the line, in the blood and in the position to receive the title and possessions that he longed for—and yet, he lost it all. However, Abel was in God's line, covered by future redeeming blood and the recipient of a heavenly inheritance.

Though Cain's name meant *acquire*, he ended up living out the meaning of Abel's name, *"vanity."* His identity was tied up in all that was *meaningless*. He had no *purpose* in his earthly life because his heart was void. He suffered the consequences, both in his earthly and eternal life because of his refusal to believe and refusal to surrender. He would not acknowledge the *glory* of God and he would not admit he needed the *grace* of God.

Though Abel's name meant *vanity*, he lived out the meaning of Cain's name, *"acquire."* He acquired all the benefits of believing and surrendering. In his earthly life, every effort he made to love and not hate, every worldly luxury he counted as meaningless (Philippians 3:8), and every struggle to resist the temporary highs of sin was well worth reaping the internal benefit of joy and completion. 1 Timothy 6:6 says, "But godliness with contentment is great gain."

Abel risked it all! Even at his death, everything Abel lost

on earth was well worth the reward and inheritance that he won for eternity!

Perhaps the best way to describe Abel's life and relationship with God is through the written words of another shepherd who would record Psalm 23: David.

> **The LORD is my shepherd,**
> **I shall not want.** (v.1 NASB)

As Abel and David were "keepers of the sheep," so was their God a "keeper" to them and so is He to us. He is a shepherd who preserves our soul as well as our life on earth for the amount of time that He purposes. He fills us completely and there is nothing we lack. We have been given access to…

- grace when we mess up
- peace when life is chaotic
- supplies when we are in need
- answers when we are clueless
- hope when we are crushed
- joy when we are sad
- strength when we are weak
- healing when our heart is broken

What more could we *want* that our Shepherd does not already promise and supply?

> **He makes me lie down in green pastures;**
> **He leads me beside quiet waters.** (v.2 NASB)

The good shepherd provides us rest in a land that is anything but barren! This pasture is rich, full and fresh because of its water supply. It's not been picked over or matted down by others. It's quality and new. Beyond that, he *makes* us rest there. His sovereign hand places us there because He knows what's good for us.

As Abel strategically led his sheep to eat and drink from the best grass and water, God led him spiritually to do the same.

> **He restores my soul;**
> **He guides me in the paths of righteousness**
> **For His name's sake.** (v.3 NASB)

He restores us back to peace from all that causes our hearts to beat out of rhythm. He is a guide and leader for us to follow and trust. We can count on Him to direct our every step in the way of truth and righteousness because this is His purpose for us. And fulfilling our purpose brings glory to His name.

In all likelihood, when Abel needed spiritual restoration, advice in a time of hardship or direction in the next steps of life, he sought the Lord who spoke truth into his heart about who he was, what he should do and which way he should go. Abel was made whole as he followed God's lead.

> **Even though I walk through the valley of**
> **the shadow of death,**
> **I fear no evil, for You are with me;**
> **Your rod and Your staff, they comfort me.**
> (v.4 NASB)

Even if we are in a deep valley facing circumstances of darkness, we can have no fear because we are not alone. God has promised us that He will never leave us or forsake us (Hebrews 13:5). Even if there is darkness all around us, we listen for His voice and we follow His light.

His rod and His staff are comforting! The rod fights off the enemy and provides us discipline and wisdom. The staff rescues us and draws us close to the Shepherd. The rod declares the Shepherds authority—His Alpha and Omega title—His glory! His staff declares His compassion—His Savior title—His grace!

No matter what issues arose in Abel's life, he counted on his ever-present God. The worst of life's circumstances did not change his belief about who God was. The glory and grace of his Shepherd was his comfort!

> **You prepare a table before me in the presence of my enemies;**
> **You have anointed my head with oil;**
> **My cup overflows.** (v.5 NASB)

Enemies often think they have cornered us and can devour us, but they are swiftly jealous, baffled and disappointed as they look down from their mountaintops and see that God has supplied a table for us to feast at in our dark valley. The anointing of our head with oil is a display of God's favor toward us. We are flooded with all of His benefits at His table. Our supply of Him is limitless!

Oh, how this is just like Cain and Abel. Cain was jealous of Abel, baffled at God's approval of him and disappointed that he could not ruin his brother's identity even by murder. Cain thought he had cornered Abel but Abel was feasting on all of God's goodness on earth and eventually in heaven.

> **Surely goodness and lovingkindness will follow me all the days of my life,**
> **And I will dwell in the house of the LORD forever.** (v.6 NASB)

No matter how many days that God has for us to live out on earth, we can trust in His goodness, love and grace. Whether on earth or in eternity, our entire mission is to declare the glory of God in His tabernacle! Our home is where His presence resides.

Truly, Abel dwelled in God's presence. He fulfilled the words, "For to me, to live is Christ and to die is gain" (Philippians 1:21 NASB). Abel became spiritually alive when he gained Christ and his physical death brought him into an eternity with Him! I think his transition from *life on earth* to *eternity in heaven* was seamless. He was believing, surrendering and praising God one moment—on one land, and he was believing, surrendering and praising Him the next moment—on another land.

Abel had gained in life and in death. He had won either way! He had gained the greatest benefit of all—an identity settled and complete in Jesus Christ! **My Life, My Death, My Gain.**

In the light of Abel's life, do the words of Psalm 23 have new meaning for you? Does this describe the way you carry out your days on earth? Do you rest in all of God's provisions? Do you feed on and drink from Him? Do you walk on His path and bring glory to His name? In the midst of all that goes wrong, are you fearless and faithful? Are His rod and His staff a comfort to you? Do you remain at His table and seek His favor over man's approval? Do you trust Him with all of your days on earth—no matter the number of them? Whether by life or death, do you seek to be in His tabernacle bringing glory to His name?

Abel's life was a living story that pictured Christ. We could go page by page of the scriptures and come up with countless individuals whose lives underwent struggles, trials and temptations and whose lives reflected love, faith and surrender. It's the same story told over and over in a different setting, in a different time period, under different circumstances and through different people. It has always been about God's story and His message of redemption.

What if even now, God wants to tell His story through you? What if the span of your life is a story of God's redeeming power? What if all that you've been through could impact others for eternity? What if you left behind an account for those to come that reflected the one true Redeemer?

The Table of Benefits

I Corinthians 10:21 says, "You cannot drink the cup of the Lord and the cup of demons; you cannot partake of the table of the Lord and the table of demons" (NASB).

I don't pretend to know what God's table and Satan's table actually look like or what material they are made of, but symbolically, I imagine it like this:

The table of Satan is fragile, **brittle** and made of glass. It exposes all your **sins**, **failures**, weaknesses and pain for you and others to see. There is no love and warmth; just a **cold** surface and a **frightful** reflection.

The plates are stained and **dirty**. Satan finds no need for napkins as he likes to cover your original identity with his filth. The utensils are **disposable** because you are not worth much to him. The cups are paper and filled with poison.

The meal is **unsatisfying**. **Discomfort** and **sickness** permeate your body from filling it with junk food. After the meal, the table breaks into a million **pieces**. As you stumble in his **darkness**, you are cut over and over. The sharp **pain** is more than you can manage and no one will help you as each man seeks only after himself. The screams and shrieks of others cause **mental insanity**. Negative emotions abound, causing frustration, **chaos** and **misery**!

Look at all the **bolded** words. This is all that Satan has to offer you. You see, Satan is not trying to trick you *at* his table. His trick is getting you *to* his table. His table represents the consequence of falling for his schemes. His deception is for you to live life at his table and suffer for eternity in his house. And eternity is a long time!

Thankfully, there is another table option. The table of God is rustic, **solid** wood. It's like the old rugged cross repurposed. It bears all sorts of notches and marks, reminding us of the many piercings that Jesus endured for us. It **covers** over a multitude of sins, pain and imperfections. The table legs are **strong** and sturdy like the Father. This table was made to last for **eternity**!

The place setting in front of each seat displays **purity** with crystal plates, white linens and silver utensils and cups. It's a proclamation that we are now **clean**. It's an affirmation of His order, our **purpose** and **security** in Him. It's a reminder of the refining process that brought us back to our **true identity**. It's a declaration of how much we are **worth** in the eyes of Christ.

God's table is a **lavish banquet**. The food on each plate is direct from His garden. No chemicals, no human errors, no cursed soil. My mouth is watering just thinking about it. The **fulfillment** of His meal spread is soul **completing**.

There is no need for a chandelier as the glory of God bursts forth with **light**. The seats provide rest and **peace**. The **communion** and **fellowship** brings **joy**. Each heart and face is filled with **love**.

What is at God's table? All the **bolded** words tell you.

God is clear about what is at His table. The benefits and rewards are beyond your imagination. You don't have to wait for your surroundings to be perfect as they will be in heaven. You can begin enjoying God's benefits now on earth! Your name is written on an invitation and all you have to do is take it.

> **One day at His table is better than a thousand days at any other!** (Psalm 84:10)

I have chosen this table. Abel chose this table. You can too!

You cannot consume from or be characterized by two different tables. No matter *who* you've been or *where* you've been, you can fully choose the table of Jesus!

You are living an earthly life drinking the cup of someone—and you will live an eternal life at someone's table. Whose cup will it be? Whose table will it be?

Only one cup can wash away your identity issues. Only one table can cover over your sins. Only one healer can mend your brokenness. There is only one God who can complete you.

Now, sit down with Him.

Believe, surrender and reap all of His benefits... *Completely!*

Acknowledgements

My husband, Joe - You inspire me more than I can explain. Thank you for supporting me in writing this book from day one! I love you.

My JJ - Thank you for bringing so much joy into my life. You will always be mama's baby! I love you!

Dad - Thank you for being my steady calm during the times I was a raging storm! I'm thankful for your godly example of faithfulness.

Mom - Thank you for chasing me down the many times I needed it. And thank you for loving me after the catch!

My other family members and friends - Thank you for your encouragement while writing this book that came at just the right moments. I am truly grateful for your love and support.

Ryan Daniel - Thank you for using your voice and talents to relay the message of having a new identity in Christ. I am more than amazed by God's orchestration of your music and this book. Thank you for your willingness to write the foreword.

Among the Thirsty - Thank you for your willingness to serve and bring glory to God through your lives and the gifts He has given you. Remain thirsty!

Linda Green - Thank you for the hours of reading and correcting my work. Your willingness is more than appreciated!

Suz Davis - Thank you for your time and interest in this project. Your insights about specific sections were enjoyable and thought provoking! Your attention to detail is amazing and I thank you for working hard at editing my work.

Diane Falco - Thank you for taking the time to read my script! Your advice was applicable and needed!

Pastor Dan Studt - Thank you for your words of wisdom as well as your time in reading and talking about specific sections of this project.

Kim Hall - Words cannot express how much your friendship means to me! Thank you for being a listening ear and an encouraging voice.

Angela Burtis - Thank you for your time, honesty and practical help on portions of this project.

Rick Policastro - Thank you for your hours of time and interest in this project. You are one talented brother-in-law! Thank you for shooting the author photo.

Toria Betelak - Thank you for your hours of fun with JJ while I edited this book! You are a wonderful cousin to him!

My readers - Thank you for your support! I pray each of you has come to the place where your heart resounds the word, *completely*.

I am most thankful to my Creator and Savior! I am completely His!

For Group or Personal Study:

#CompletelyBook
#CompletelyHis

The Beginning, The End

The beginning tells us about the end. The one who is Alpha, is Omega. The Alpha and Omega is none other than our Lord and Savior! He has made us in His image and given us His breathe of life. Don't let Satan convince you of a subtraction of your identity. There is nothing to gain apart from God.

Do you believe in God's identity from the beginning? Do you believe in what God says is true about your identity from the beginning? Have you been recreated by the Potter? What subtraction of God's identity or your identity is Satan tempting you to believe in? When you've fallen for that temptation, what "addition" did you acquire?

My Shepherd, My Direction

If we follow the good Shepherd, He will lead us down the right path. We must be willing to listen to Him.

Do you welcome the leading of God as well as godly people in your life—or do you tend to think you have all the answers on your own? Whose wisdom do you seek? How do you shepherd your children?

My Faith: Past and Future, My Faith: Present

We can live out faith in any present moment by resting on what God did in the past and by trusting in what He promises for the future.

How are you living out your present moments? By faith or by crisis? What part of your past or what unknowns of your future do you need to surrender so you can live out a better present? How does living by crisis affect your offerings to the Lord?

My Treasure, My Heart

What we treasure the most, we store in our heart. Our treasure and our heart are inseparable.

What negative emotions or poor character traits in Cain can you relate to? What worldly treasures need to be removed from your heart? What emotions are often revealed on your face? Which fruits need more growth in your life? Have you taken up the full armor of God?

Change My Treasure, Change My Heart

If we want to change our heart, we need to change what we treasure. We need to give up the lifeless god of ourselves in exchange for the living God of the universe! We need to take our first spiritual breath by breathing in God and breathing out self. This type of breathing is how we continue to live well.

Who is your God? Have you trusted in the One who has conquered the enemy? Is God calling you to do something that is impossible to do without Him? How will you respond to Him? How is your breathing? What part of God are you not believing? What part of self are you holding on to?

My Heart, My Words

The treasures we store in our heart flow out through our words.

What words does your heart speak? What treasures need to leave your heart so that you can honor God with your words? Do you allow the words of others to affect the words you respond with? Do you seek to control the behavior of others or influence their heart-change?

My Heart, My Actions

The treasures we store in our heart flow out in our actions.

Do you keep or kill those around you? How can you be a better keeper of your brother? How can you be more aware of those who need keeping? What/Who needs more preserving in your life? What needs more creativity? How can you balance the two? How would eliminating earthly treasures in your heart make you a better keeper of those around you?

Surrender the Old, Receive the New

We need the powerful blood of Christ to cover our sins. The cross is the place where we can surrender the old and receive the new. It's a place where we can make a swap.

What do you need to surrender at the cross? What benefit will you receive as a result? Have you received the mark of eternal preservation?

My Life, My Legacy

The way we live our lives will leave a legacy for those to come.

What is God calling you to do that will impact future generations? What testimony will you leave behind?

Who God Is, Who I Am

God's identity tells us about our identity. When we completely believe in and surrender to who He is, we experience the fullness of who we truly are in Him!

What are you doubting or resisting? What effects does your doubt or resistance have on your life? What truth of God's identity do you need to focus on? What truth of your identity are you not living out?

God's Glory, God's Grace

There is nothing so good about us that can match God's glory and there's nothing so bad about us that God's grace can't cover! Your worth is not in your abilities. Your worth is found in Him!

Are you attempting to gain your worth outside of Christ? What weakness or effect of the curse are you holding onto like an idol? Will you let go of your insecurity? Will your heart resound, "Completely?"

My Life, My Death, My Gain

Whether we are living for God on earth or praising Him in heaven, there is no greater gain than Christ.

What is the span of your life truly about? Are you fulfilling who God made you to be? Whose table are you sitting at? What are the benefits of believing and surrendering completely?

Endnotes

1 "By permission. From *Merriam-Webster's Collegiate® Dictionary, 11th Edition* ©2016 by Merriam-Webster, Inc. ([http://www.Merriam-Webster.com)]www.Merriam-Webster.com)."

2 Strong, James. 1890. Strong's Exhaustive Concordance of the Bible. New York, Eaton & Mains; Cincinnati, Jennings & Graham.

3 Spurgeon, Charles. "The Metropolitan Tabernacle Pulpit: Sermons", (Passmore & Alabaster, 1879), 98.

4 from Thayer's Greek Lexicon, PC Study Bible formatted Electronic Database. Copyright © 2006 by Biblesoft, Inc. All rights reserved.

5 from Thayer's Greek Lexicon, PC Study Bible formatted Electronic Database. Copyright © 2006 by Biblesoft, Inc. All rights reserved.

6 Strong, James. 1890. Strong's Exhaustive Concordance of the Bible. New York, Eaton & Mains; Cincinnati, Jennings & Graham.

7 from Thayer's Greek Lexicon, PC Study Bible formatted Electronic Database. Copyright © 2006 by Biblesoft, Inc. All rights reserved.

8 Strong, James. 1890. Strong's Exhaustive Concordance of the Bible. New York, Eaton & Mains; Cincinnati, Jennings & Graham.

9 Copyright © 2014 Universal Music - Brentwood Benson Publ. (ASCAP) Kiss The Muse Music (ASCAP) (adm. at CapitolCMGpublishing.com) / We R Younger We R Faster () All rights reserved. Used by permission.
© 2014 We Are Younger We Are Faster/ASCAP (Administered by Music Services) / Brentwood Benson Publishing / Kiss The Muse Music. All Rights Reserved. Used By Permission.

10 Strong, James. 1890. Strong's Exhaustive Concordance of the Bible. New York, Eaton & Mains; Cincinnati, Jennings & Graham.

11 Wesley Center for Applied Theology of Northwest Nazarene University, Nampa, Idaho. https://wesley.nnu.edu/john-wesley/john-wesley-the-methodist/chapter-vi-to-america-and-back/.

12 Wesley Center for Applied Theology of Northwest Nazarene University, Nampa, Idaho. https:// wesley.nnu.edu/charles-wesley/the-journal-of-charles-welsey-1707-1788/the-journal-of-charles-wesley-may-1-august-31-1738/.

13 Wesley Center for Applied Theology of Northwest Nazarene University, Nampa, Idaho. https:// wesley.nnu.edu/charles-wesley/the-journal-of-charles-welsey-1707-1788/the-journal-of-charles-wesley-may-1-august-31-1738/.

14 Wesley Center for Applied Theology of Northwest Nazarene University, Nampa, Idaho. https://wesley.nnu.edu/charles-wesley/the-journal-of-charles-welsey-1707-1788/the-journal-of-charles-wesley-may-1-august-31-1738/.

15 Wesley Center for Applied Theology of Northwest Nazarene University, Nampa, Idaho. https://wesley.nnu.edu/john-wesley/john-wesley-the-methodist/chapter-vii-the-new-birth/.

16 Wesley, Charles. And Can It Be, That I Should Gain?. 1738.

17 Wesley, Charles. And Can It Be, That I Should Gain?. 1738.

18 Wesley, Charles. And Can It Be, That I Should Gain?. 1738.

19 Strong, James. 1890. Strong's Exhaustive Concordance of the Bible. New York, Eaton & Mains; Cincinnati, Jennings & Graham.

20 Strong, James. 1890. Strong's Exhaustive Concordance of the Bible. New York, Eaton & Mains; Cincinnati, Jennings & Graham.

21 The Discovery Bible New Testament, Gary Hill, 2014.

22 The Discovery Bible New Testament, Gary Hill, 2014.

23 Strong, James. 1890. Strong's Exhaustive Concordance of the Bible. New York, Eaton & Mains; Cincinnati, Jennings & Graham.

24 Strong, James. 1890. Strong's Exhaustive Concordance of the Bible. New York, Eaton & Mains; Cincinnati, Jennings & Graham.

25 Strong, James. 1890. Strong's Exhaustive Concordance of the Bible. New York, Eaton & Mains; Cincinnati, Jennings & Graham.

26 from Thayer's Greek Lexicon, PC Study Bible formatted Electronic Database. Copyright © 2006 by Biblesoft, Inc. All rights reserved.

27 PIERRE DUMAS HIS LIFE and HIS DESCENDANTS 1756 to 1986, Hallie Arden DeMass Sweeting, R.D. 2, Sterling, New York 1986.

28 PIERRE DUMAS HIS LIFE and HIS DESCENDANTS 1756 to 1986, Hallie Arden DeMass Sweeting, R.D. 2, Sterling, New York 1986.

29 Billy Graham, Greenville, SC, 1966.

30 Strong, James. 1890. Strong's Exhaustive Concordance of the Bible. New York, Eaton & Mains; Cincinnati, Jennings & Graham.

[31] Lemmel, Helen H. Turn Your Eyes upon Jesus. 1922

[32] Strong, James. 1890. Strong's Exhaustive Concordance of the Bible. New York, Eaton & Mains; Cincinnati, Jennings & Graham.

[33] Babcock, Maltbie D. This is My Father's World. 1901.

[34] Strong, James. 1890. Strong's Exhaustive Concordance of the Bible. New York, Eaton & Mains; Cincinnati, Jennings & Graham.

[35] Strong, James. 1890. Strong's Exhaustive Concordance of the Bible. New York, Eaton & Mains; Cincinnati, Jennings & Graham.

[36] Strong, James. 1890. Strong's Exhaustive Concordance of the Bible. New York, Eaton & Mains; Cincinnati, Jennings & Graham.

Printed in the United States
By Bookmasters